IT'S CHRISTMAS!

EASY AND FESTIVE
DO-IT-AHEAD
MENUS AND RECIPES

First printing September 1989
10,000 copies
Second printing January 1991
10,000 copies
Third printing May 1994
5,000 copies
Deanne II, Inc.
#3 Quail Run
Box 82A, Rt. 4
Carthage, Missouri 64836

ISBN 0-9611584-1-7
Cover Design and Division
HOLLY FORBES

Illustrations
ELAINA STOCK EDMAN

Printed in the USA by
WIMMER
The Wimmer Companies, Inc.
Memphis • Dallas

FOREWORD

To the foresighted hostess searching for imaginative yuletide menus and very special party ideas, the co-authors of RUSH HOUR SUPERCHEF offer an exciting and different kind of cookbook.

From treasured family recipes of the traditional foods of Christmas, and intriguing new ones to add a little extra flourish, they have evolved a wealth of delectable and festive menus to fit every holiday get-together.

Take a look and chart your course! Whether it's a few friends dropping in to bolster spirits with a cup of egg nog, or a gala open house for friends and neighbors, the formula for a merry, merry Christmas is the same. Get ready ahead of time! Plan! Shop! Freeze!

From the sentimental family tree-trimming with simple and hearty soups and pasta, to the wondrous Christmas feast with its three choices—the traditional, the Victorian, the lavish buffet, ten chapters ablaze with holiday hospitality and step-by-step directions await the hostess.

There's even a fun and games chapter called, "All Aboard! Here Comes the Kindergarten Bunch!"

A wreathful of Christmas traditions to all who read this book.

Dianne Stafford Mayes
and
Dorothy Davenport Stafford

TABLE OF

IT'S CHRISTMAS!
Imaginative Menus Ablaze with Holiday Hospitality

"Be merry all, be merry all,
With holly dress the festive hall,
Prepare the song, the feast, the ball,
To welcome Merry Christmas."

William Spencer

CONTENTS

A Merry Christmas Tree Trimming

Holiday enchantment reigns! It's the night the family gathers to trim the tall tree standing in its accustomed place by the window, green and bare. They're all there, from the oldest uncle and aunt to the youngest kindergartner. The big boxes of tree ornaments have been opened, their contents scattered in bright disarray on chairs and sofa.

Lambs for the créche, golden balls, silver bells, angels in tarnished tinsel, a shining gold star for the top of the tree, special treasured ornaments from far away places, all evoking a chorus of "Do you remember?"

Three easy-to-do menus are suggested, each with a main dish prepared ahead and kept piping hot on an electric hot plate or left simmering on the kitchen cooktop for dawdling eaters. Though grown-ups may begin serving themselves early, the children, eyes wide with wonder, are happily preoccupied with where to put the angel riding a shooting star or the beloved wooden Santa Claus.

A MERRY CHRISTMAS TREE TRIMMING

Do-It Ahead Buffet

A MERRY CHRISTMAS TREE TRIMMING

Do-It Ahead Buffet

Christmas Pasta
Crusty Hard Rolls
Tangerines, Apples, and Grape Clusters
Ice Cream
and/or
Tray of Assorted Christmas Cookies

Lentil and Frankfurter Soup
Assorted Crackers and Cheeses
Grape Clusters
Popcorn and Ice Cream Bars

Hearty Yuletide Stew
Toasted Cornbread Squares
Fresh Pears and Apple Wedges
Christmas Pound Cake

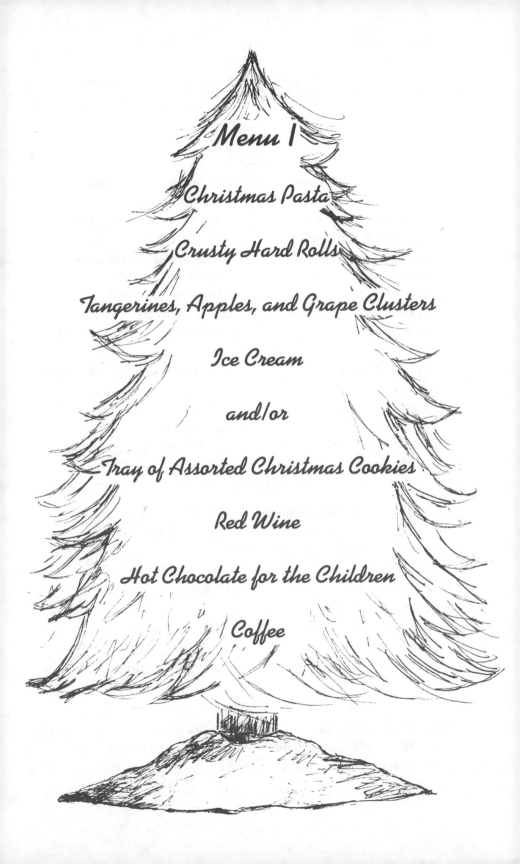

Menu I

Christmas Pasta

Crusty Hard Rolls

Tangerines, Apples, and Grape Clusters

Ice Cream

and/or

Tray of Assorted Christmas Cookies

Red Wine

Hot Chocolate for the Children

Coffee

Christmas Pasta or Rigatoni al Forno

Deliciosa!…Freezes Well
Serves 8-10

SAUCE

2 cups finely chopped white onion or ½ cup dried instant onion
1 large clove garlic finely minced
1 t. dried basil or 1 T. finely chopped fresh basil
½ t. crushed dried sage
1 t. oregano

⅛ t. ground red pepper or ¼ t. Tabasco
2 14½ ounce cans peeled whole Italian tomatoes, undrained (Contadina preferred)
1 cup chicken broth (Swanson's preferred, freeze remainder of can)

• • • • • • • • • • •

1 pound mild Italian sausage (Papa Scavuzzo's recommended)
1 T. olive oil
½ pound fresh

mushrooms, quartered if large mushrooms
1½ T. butter or butter substitute
1 garlic clove pressed or finely minced

CHEESE FILLING

2 cups fresh Ricotta cheese (can substitute well drained creamy cottage cheese)
2 beaten eggs
½ cup chopped fresh

parsley (or 4 T. dried parsley flakes)
1 t. salt
½ t. coarsely ground black pepper

• • • • • • • • • • •

6 T. freshly grated Parmesan cheese

2 cups shredded Mozzarella cheese

PASTA

1 16 ounce package Rigatoni (can substitute 12 Lasagna noodles)

1 T. olive oil
6 cups boiling water

SAUCE PREPARATION

1. In a large saucepan put chopped onions, minced garlic, basil, sage, oregano, red pepper, undrained tomatoes, and chicken broth.
2. Bring to a boil, reduce heat to medium low, and let simmer 30 minutes or until liquid is reduced in half. Stir occasionally.
3. While sauce is simmering, remove casings from sausage. In a frying pan, cook sausage in 1 T. olive oil until done and sausage has rendered all of its fat.
4. Drain thoroughly. When cool crumble sausage and set aside.
5. Melt 1½ T. butter in skillet. Add pressed or finely minced garlic clove. Let garlic simmer in butter for a minute.
6. Add mushrooms and cook over medium heat, stirring constantly, 4 to 5 minutes or until mushrooms are tender crisp. If cooking mushrooms in microwave, cook 1 minute 20 seconds, stirring after 1 minute.
7. Remove from heat, set aside, leaving mushrooms in liquid until ready to use.
8. When sauce has finished cooking, drain mushrooms. Stir crumbled sausage and mushrooms into sauce. Simmer for 5 minutes. Remove from heat and set aside.

CHEESE FILLING PREPARATION

1. Mix together Ricotta, parsley, eggs, salt and pepper.
2. Whip by hand or in mixer until creamy and well blended. Set aside.

PASTA PREPARATION

1. Bring 6 cups water and 1 T. olive oil to a boil.
2. Add 1 16 oz. package Rigatoni or 12 Lasagna noodles.
3. Reduce heat and cook 12 minutes only.
4. Drain in colander and rinse with cold water.

Continued on next page

TO ASSEMBLE

1. Preheat oven to 375 degrees.
2. Lightly butter an 8 x 12 or 9 x 13 pyrex baking dish.
3. Spread one half of the sauce over the bottom.
4. Cover with half the cooked rigatoni.
5. Cover with half the cheese filling.
6. Sprinkle half the mozzarella and 3 T. Parmesan over cheese filling.
7. Repeat layers.*
8. Bake 375 degrees for 30 minutes or until hot and bubbly throughout. Can run under broiler for a couple of minutes to give Rigatoni a golden brown glaze.
9. Let sit 10-15 minutes before cutting in squares. Serve with crusty hard rolls and fruit.

*If freezing, do not bake. Wrap tightly in aluminum foil then in freezer wrap and place in freezer. Let come to room temperature before cooking.

Crusty Hard Rolls

Buy number of rolls needed at grocery or deli. Heat for 10 minutes at 325. Serve warm with butter.

Tangerines, Apples, and Grape Clusters

1. Arrange fruit attractively on tray. Cut apples, sprinkle with fruit fresh, p. 20, half peel tangerines, and cut grapes in clusters. Intersperse grape clusters among tangerines and apples. Cover & refrigerate until ready to serve.

Ice Cream and/or Tray of Assorted Christmas Cookies

Purchase your family's favorite ice cream and surprise them with an assortment of Christmas cookies from your freezer— pages 167-174.

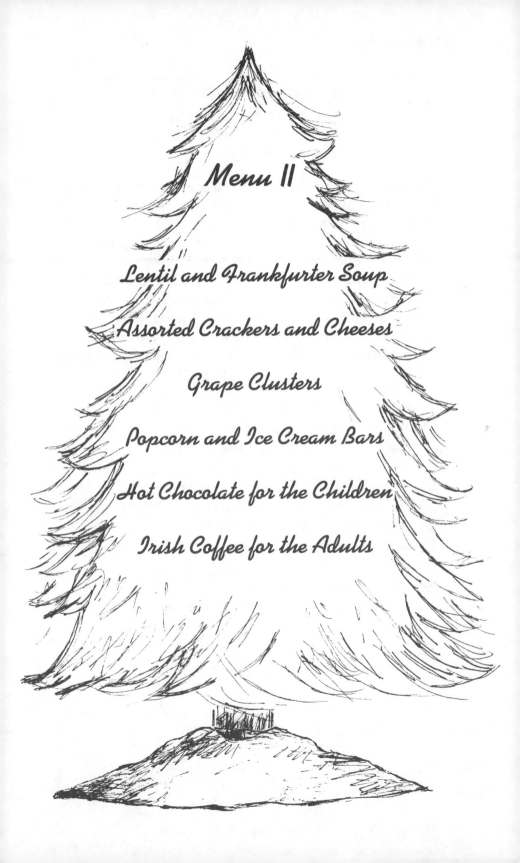

Menu II

Lentil and Frankfurter Soup

Assorted Crackers and Cheeses

Grape Clusters

Popcorn and Ice Cream Bars

Hot Chocolate for the Children

Irish Coffee for the Adults

Lentil and Frankfurter Soup

A Trim-The-Tree Favorite
Make Ahead — Freezes Well
Serves 8

1 T. olive oil or corn oil
1 16 ounce package
  frankfurters (can use
  turkey franks if preferred)
1 cup celery, chopped
½ cup green pepper,
  chopped
1 cup carrots, chopped
1 clove garlic, pressed or
  finely minced

1 16 ounce package navy
  beans, rinsed
2 14½ ounce cans
  Swansons Beef Broth
6 cups hot water
1 16 oz. can Rotel tomatoes
  (optional, add if you want
  soup to be fairly spicy)
3 whole bay leaves
¼ t. coarsely ground black
  pepper

1. Slice franks ¼ inch thick in pieces.
2. Heat oil in a 4 quart pan and brown franks on all sides. Remove and refrigerate until ready to use.
3. Put celery, green pepper, carrots, and garlic in same pan. Sauté for 10 minutes, stirring. Remove from heat.
4. Add beans, beef broth, water, tomatoes (optional), pepper, and bay leaves to pan with vegetables.
5. Cover and cook 2 hours on medium low or until beans are soft.
6. Remove bay leaves and serve warm or put into airtight containers and freeze until ready to serve.

Assorted Crackers and Cheeses with Grape Clusters

(Prepare cheese tray ahead of time and add grape clusters at last minute. Cheese should be at room temperature for full flavor)
Estimated amounts for 8 people

6-8 ounces Monterey Jack or Munster
6-8 ounces aged Cheddar

1 pound grapes
Assortment of thin crisp crackers

1. Wash and dry grapes. Cut into small clusters. Refrigerate until ready to use.
2. Arrange cheese attractively on tray with crackers to the side. Cover and set aside until ready to serve.
3. At serving time, place clusters of grapes among the cheeses and crackers, decorate with parsley and let everyone help themselves.

Popcorn and Ice Cream Bars

1. Buy ice cream bars at grocery and keep in freezer until ready to serve.
2. Pop corn earlier in day and keep tightly covered. Heat in a 300 degree oven for 10-15 minutes before serving.

Irish Coffee

A cup of cheer after all the hard work
See p. 207 for recipe

Menu III

Hearty Yuletide Stew

Toasted Cornbread Squares

Fresh Pears and Apple Wedges

Christmas Pound Cake

Hot Chocolate
(for the children)

Red or White Wine

Coffee

Hearty Yuletide Stew or Boeuf À La Bourguigonne

Make a day or two ahead or a month in advance and freeze—
stew gains in flavor when reheated.

Serves 6-8

**1 cup chopped cooked
bacon (about 12 pieces
thick sliced bacon)
3 pounds lean chuck, cut
into 1 to 1½ inch cubes
½ t. salt
½ coarsely ground black**

**pepper
½ t. Knorr Swiss Aromat
All Purpose Seasoning
(optional, but adds
flavor)
2 T. all purpose flour**

• • • • • • • • • • •

**2 cups sliced onions
(1 large onion)**

**4 medium carrots, cut
into chunks
½ cup Brandy (optional)**

• • • • • • • • • • •

**2 cloves garlic minced
1 bay leaf crumbled
½ t. thyme
1 T. tomato paste**

**2 cups (1 14½ ounce can)
Swansons Clear Beef
Broth
3 cups Burgundy or a full
bodied dry red wine**

• • • • • • • • • • •

**20-24 small white onions,
skinned (If you cannot
find baby onions, buy the
smallest onions you can
find and allow 1 to
2 onions per person.
Purchase onions
similar in size)
½ pound fresh
mushrooms quartered**

**2 T. butter or butter
substitute
1 T. olive oil
⅛ t. salt
⅛ t. pepper
1 t. lemon juice
½ cup chopped parsley
(optional)**

1. Preheat oven to 325 degrees.
2. Sauté bacon in a large skillet until brown. Remove bacon
   and drain on paper towel, reserving bacon drippings in
   pan.
3. In a mixing bowl, mix together salt, pepper, Knoor
   seasoning, and flour. Stir until well blended.

Continued on next page

4. Add cubed beef and toss until all cubes are lightly coated.

5. Add half of beef cubes to skillet and sauté on medium heat until cubes are brown on all sides. Remove and drain on a paper towel. Repeat with rest of beef.

• • • • • • • • • • • •

1. In the same skillet, sauté until lightly browned the sliced onions and carrot chunks.

2. Add the brandy (optional), stir to mix thoroughly with rest of ingredients, light with a match when hot, and let simmer until flame dies out. The alcohol will evaporate, leaving only the flavor to enhance the dish.

3. With a slotted spoon, remove the onions and carrots to a large casserole or dutch oven.

4. Add cubed beef and crumbled bacon.

• • • • • • • • • • • •

1. To the casserole add: minced garlic cloves, crumbled bay leaf, thyme, tomato paste, 1 can Swanson's beef broth, and 3 cups Burgundy.

2. Stir to mix well.

3. Place, covered, in a 325 degree oven. Cook for 2½ to 3 hours. Meat is done when it can be pierced easily with a fork. • • • • • • • • • • • •

1. While beef is cooking, prepare mushrooms and onions. To freeze the stew, do not cook onions and mushrooms until serving day.

2. In a 2 quart saucepan, cover onions with water. Bring to a boil, reduce heat to medium and cook approximately 8 to 10 minutes for tiny baby onions and 15 to 20 minutes for larger onions. IMPORTANT—test with a pronged fork. Onions should be "tender crisp"—NOT SOFT. Remove and let drain on a paper towel. Set aside until ready to use.

3. Quarter mushrooms, reserving stems.

4. Melt 2 T. butter and 1 T. oil in skillet. Add salt, pepper, lemon juice, and mushrooms. Sauté over medium heat, stirring, until mushrooms are barely done—about 2 to 3 minutes.

5. Remove from skillet and set aside along with onions until ready to use.

6. Have optional chopped parsley set aside.

Continued on next page

WHEN STEW IS READY

1. Remove from oven and distribute cooked onions and mushrooms over meat.
2. Simmer several minutes, basting mushrooms and onions with sauce several times or until mushrooms and onions are hot. Sprinkle chopped parsley over top.
3. Serve in warm soup bowls. For a "Trim the Tree" evening, leave stew barely simmering on the cooktop or place on an electric hot tray and let the family eat whenever one is hungry. Serve with cornbread squares and fruit.

IF FROZEN—let stew come to room temperature, put in casserole or dutch oven, and simmer 15 to 20 minutes until heated throughout. Baste occasionally with sauce.

Toasted Cornbread Squares

Make ahead and freeze
Makes 12 squares

1 8½ ounce box "Jiffy" corn muffin mix
1 T. butter

1 egg
⅓ cup milk

1. Preheat oven to 400 degrees.
2. Place 1 T. butter in an 8 x 8 baking dish. Place dish in oven and let butter melt.
3. Remove from oven and paint sides and bottom of baking dish with butter.
4. In a small bowl, mix together corn muffin mix, egg, and milk. Stir until well blended—batter will be lumpy.
5. Pour evenly into baking dish, place in oven and bake 20 to 25 minutes. Test at end of 20 minutes with toothpick or broom straw. Toothpick should be clean with no batter adhering to it when stuck in center of cornbread.
6. Remove from oven and cut in squares.
7. Split each square in two, lightly butter tops, and run under broiler until crispy and brown on top—delicious!

Fresh Pears and Apples

Prepare early in the day and refrigerate

1. Allow one half apple and one half pear per person—more if you are feeding a hungry group.
2. Quarter apples and pears and then cut each wedge again in half.
3. Place fruit in separate containers, saturate with Fruit Fresh syrup (see following recipe), cover tightly with plastic wrap, and refrigerate until ready to use.
4. At serving time, arrange attractively on a platter alongside Yuletide Stew and Cornbread Squares.

Fruit Fresh Syrup

(for preserving fresh fruits)

(makes enough for 1 qt. of fruit)

2 t. Fruit Fresh   **3 T. water**

1. Dissolve Fruit Fresh in water and toss with 1 quart of fruit.
2. Refrigerate in air tight containers until ready to use.
3. At serving time, drain any syrup or accumulated liquid from fruit.

Christmas Pound Cake

The "Make Ahead Christmas Surprise"
See p. 178, 179 for recipe

WELCOME! A HOLIDAY OPEN HOUSE!
...'TIS THE SEASON OF PARTIES...

Swing wide the portals of hospitality to those who knock and enter...a house alight with the warm glow of candles, festive food, and holiday spirits.

WELCOME! A HOLIDAY OPEN HOUSE! FESTIVE FOOD AND YULETIDE CHEER

Christmas Antipasto Tray
Toasted Crab Salad Finger Puffs
Roast of Sirloin
with
Bearnaise Sauce
Festive Cheese and Fruit Board
Crackers and Melba Toast Rounds
Tempting Assortment of Cookies and Candies

Sweet and Sour Meatballs
Savory Shrimp Mold
Garden Fresh Vegetable Tray
choice of
Five Minute Dip...Curry Lovers Dip...Creamy Dill
Zesty Onion Sandwiches
Fresh Apple Slices and Pear Wedges
served with
Chutney Blue Cheese
Fruit Cake Slices and Assorted Cookies

Carolina Cheese Biscuits
Succulent Assorted Cold Cuts
Potato Rolls and Party Rye
Scalloped Crab
with
Melba Toast Rounds
Cocoanut Chutney Cheese Spread
Fruit Bowl
of
Green Cherry Pineapple Spears and Frosted Grapes

Menu I

Christmas Antipasto Tray

Toasted Crab Salad Finger Puffs

Roast of Sirloin

with

Bearnaise Sauce

Potato Rolls and Party Rye

Festive Cheese and Fruit Board

Crackers and Melba Toast Rounds

Tempting Assortment of Christmas Cookies

and Candies

Christmas Antipasto Tray

Assemble early in the day, cover, and refrigerate until ready to
serve

Rolled Stuffed Salami

**Deviled Eggs Garnished
  with Pimento Strips**

Herbed Cherry Tomatoes

Marinated Artichoke Hearts

**Marinated Mushroom
  Buttons**

**Red and Green Pepper
  Strips**

Ripe Olives

Stuffed Green Olives

Parsley

Party Toothpicks

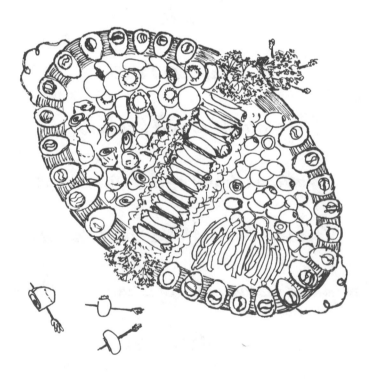

Rolled Stuffed Salami

Can make three to four days before and refrigerate or a month before and freeze—if frozen, place in an airtight container and wrap well with freezer paper.
Makes 28—Allow two per person

2 4 oz. boxes Hormel Party Salami (or equivalent amount of any thin sliced, cooked salami)
1 8 oz. package cream cheese, room temperature

3 t. horseradish
2½ t. lemon juice
2½ T. mayonnaise
1 chopped green pepper (optional)
Party toothpicks with frills

1. Combine softened cream cheese, horseradish, lemon juice, mayonnaise, and green pepper in small mixing bowl.
2. Mix with fork until well combined.
3. Spread each salami slice with heaping teaspoon of cream cheese mixture.
4. Roll up and secure with toothpick.
5. Cover tightly with foil and refrigerate.
6. At serving time, place on tray and garnish with parsley.

Deviled Eggs

(Take your choice of the two recipes offered—
make several days in advance)
See Rule, p. 229, "How to Hard Boil Eggs"

Deviled Eggs I

Makes 24 halves

12 hard cooked eggs
¼ cup plus 2 T.
 mayonnaise or "lite"
 mayonnaise
¼ cup Durkee Sandwich
and Salad Sauce

1 T. cider vinegar plus 2 t.
¼-½ t. salt
¼ t. coarsely ground black
 pepper

1. Peel and slice eggs lengthwise.
2. Remove yolks with a spoon and place in mixing bowl. Mash with a fork or potato masher.
3. Add mayonnaise, Durkee's, vinegar, ¼ t. salt, and ¼ t. pepper. Beat by hand or with electric mixer until all ingredients are well combined and mixture is light and fluffy.
4. Taste and add other ¼ t. salt if needed.
5. Mound mixture into egg whites.
6. Sprinkle with paprika and vary with the following garnishes: Pimento strips, sliced green olives, and sliced black olives with a sprig of parsley in center.
7. Cover tightly and refrigerate until ready to serve.

Deviled Eggs II

Makes 24 halves

12 hard cooked eggs
1 cup mayonnaise or "light
mayonnaise"

1 T. Horseradish-Mustard

1. Peel and slice eggs lengthwise.
2. Remove yolks with a spoon and place in mixing bowl. Mash with a fork or a potato masher.
3. Add mayonnaise and horseradish-mustard. Beat by hand or with an electric mixer until all ingredients are well combined and mixture is light and fluffy.
4. Mound mixture into egg whites.
5. Sprinkle with paprika and vary with the following garnishes: sliced ripe olives with pimento strips, and sliced, stuffed green olives.
6. Cover tightly and refrigerate until ready to serve.

Herbed Cherry Tomatoes

Can be prepared day before
Serves 20-24

2 pints cherry tomatoes
1 cup olive oil
¼ t. salt

¼ t. oregano
2 garlic cloves pressed or
mashed with a fork

1. Wash and stem tomatoes. Cut in half and pat dry.
2. Combine olive oil, seasonings, and garlic in a bowl. Stir to mix well.
3. Add cherry tomatoes, tossing to coat well.
4. Let marinate 2 to 4 hours or overnight.
5. Drain well and serve either cold or at room temperature.

Marinated Artichoke Hearts

(Can be drained and stored in refrigerator day before)
Serves 14-16 allowing for 1 to 2 artichokes per person

**2 6 ounce jars marinated
artichoke hearts**

1. Drain artichoke hearts and place on paper towel to absorb most of oil.
2. Cut each whole artichoke heart in fourths.
3. Refrigerate in air tight container until ready to use.

Marinated Mushroom Buttons

Prepare Ahead—can be drained and stored
in refrigerator day before
Serves 18-20 allowing for 1 to 2 buttons per person

**2 6 ounce jars Marinated
Mushroom Buttons**

1. Drain mushroom buttons and place on paper towel to absorb most of marinade.
2. Store in air tight container in refrigerator until ready to use.

Red and Green Pepper Strips

Prepare day before.
These are mainly for garnish. If your guests enjoy a crunchy
strip of green pepper, increase amount.
Serves 20-24

1 green bell pepper   1 red bell pepper

1. Wash and pat dry peppers.
2. Cut in half and remove seeds and membrane.
3. Cut in thin strips, wrap in moist paper towels or dampened dish towel, and store in air tight container or ziploc bag in refrigerator until ready to serve.

Ripe and Stuffed Green Olives

Prepare Ahead
Olives are an additional and attractive garnish for the
Antipasto Tray—Sprinkle them generously around and over
the top of the antipasto.

1 jar ripe olives   **1 jar stuffed green olives**

1. Drain and pat dry.
2. Arrange attractively among the various food items offered
   on the tray.

Toasted Crab Salad Finger Puffs

Allow 2-3 rolls per each guest—so delicious they disappear
quickly
Makes 20 individual rolls

1 lb. lump crab meat   **½ t. Tabasco**
4 T. fresh lemon juice   **½ t. Light Salt**
2 cups finely diced celery   **1 package of 20 Pepperidge**
1 cup mayonnaise (no   **Farm Enriched Party**
    substitute except "lite"   **Rolls**
    mayonnaise)

1. Remove any remaining shells or cartilage from crab meat.
2. Put in mixing bowl and add: lemon juice, celery,
   mayonnaise, Tabasco, & salt.
3. With a sharp knife cut out center of each party roll and
   place on cookie sheet large enough to hold 20 or more
   rolls.
4. Stuff each roll generously with crab salad, and store in
   refrigerator covered with damp cloth until ready to serve.
5. Turn oven to 300 degrees and cook approximately 20
   minutes. Caution: Be sure rolls are hot when served. (Can
   be kept warm on electric buffet hot tray.)

Roast of Sirloin

A more expensive cut of meat, but more economical in the long run because of no waste.
A 7 pound roast will serve 30-35 people 3 party size sandwiches each. Cook and slice the day before.

1 Sirloin Roast (not sirloin tip)—have butcher leave a small amount of fat on one side.

Coarsely ground black pepper
1 clove garlic
Potato rolls and Party Rye

1. Preheat oven to 550 degrees. Have roast at room temperature.
2. Rub roast with 1 clove garlic and coarsely ground black pepper.
3. Place in roaster or shallow baking dish uncovered, fat side up and put in oven.
4. Immediately turn oven down to 325 degrees.
5. Cook:

DONENESS	MINUTES PER POUND	MEAT THERMOMETER WILL READ
RARE	18-22 minutes	140 degrees
MEDIUM	25 minutes	155-160 degrees
WELL DONE	33 minutes	170 degrees

Rule of thumb for a party is to serve meat medium rare—22 minutes per pound should be a good gauge, but a meat thermometer is always the most reliable.
6. Remove from oven, let sit 10 minutes for easier carving.
7. Slice paper thin, wrap in foil, and refrigerate until ready to serve.
8. Let come to room temperature before serving. Place on a large serving platter, garnish liberally with parsley, and serve with warm Bearnaise Sauce. Option: add a small bowl of mayonnaise for those not wishing Bearnaise Sauce.
9. Place a tray of potato rolls and a basket of party rye to each side of roast.

The Best of the Best Bearnaise Sauce

Prepare Ahead.
Will keep a week or two in refrigerator. Also freezes well. If
frozen, do not cook to thicken until ready to use.
Makes 1 cup.

PART I

2 T. chicken broth
2 T. tarragon vinegar

¾ t. bottled lemon juice or
1 T. fresh lemon juice
3 T. chopped green onions
(tops included)

PART II

3 egg yolks
½ cup butter (1 stick),
   softened
2 sprays celery leaves
2 sprigs parsley

½ t. salt
⅛ t. coarsely ground black
   pepper
¼ t. Tabasco

1. Bring all ingredients in Part I to a boil.
2. Place all ingredients in Part II in blender and run at medium
   speed.
3. Slowly pour hot mixture (Part I) into blender while running.
   Mix well.
4. Cook over hot water until sauce thickens—about 3-4
   minutes, stirring constantly.

Festive Cheese and Fruit Board

Cheese and parties go together naturally—add crunchy apples and clusters of fresh grapes for an elegant and easy addition to the buffet table. Offer at least three types of cheese, varying in flavor from mild to sharp in texture from creamy to firm. Choose cheeses of different colors and shapes; cut some in wedges, bars, or chunks for variety. If possible, taste the cheese before you buy it—most cheeses will vary greatly in flavor. Serve at room temperature for full flavor.

SUGGESTED CHEESE-BOARD ASSORTMENTS

Purchase 6 ounces of each cheese
Will serve 10-12

BRIE
(soft, ripened, delicate, and indescribably delicious)

GORGONZOLA
Most delicate of all the natural blues. When young, it is semi-soft, almost creamy and utterly delightful. Italian in origin, a good imitation is produced in Wisconsin.

EDAM
The Dutch "cannon ball" cheese, with a bright red outer rind and a firm, golden interior. Intended mainly for cutting in wedges.

• • • • • • • • • • •

PORT SALUT
A world renown semi-soft cheese made by the Trappist monks of Notre Dame in France since 1816

SAMSO
One of the finest of Danish cheeses. Semi-firm, with a nut-like buttery flavor.

AGED CHEDDAR
Sharp and firm.

BOURSIN
A French triple cream cheese, soft and delicious. See recipe p. 34 for "Domestic Boursin"

BABY SWISS
Semi firm—Swiss is the name commonly used in the United States for the big holed cheese. Originating in the 15th century in the Emmantal Valley in Switzerland, it is known in Switzerland and other European countries as Emmentaler.

DANISH BLUE
The sharpest of the blues—cut in wedges.

• • • • • • • • • • •

CRÈME de GRUYÈRE
Soft ripened French cheese with the flavor of Gruyere, but the consistency of Camembert. Delicious as a spread for crackers or a topping for fresh fruit slices.

MUNSTER
A mild, semi firm, buttery like cheese with a distinctive flavor— especially good accompanied with apples or nuts.

AGED BABY GOUDA
Of Dutch origin, round in shape with a red rind. A nice contrast in taste and texture to the above two.

• • • • • • • • • • •

These are only suggestions. Ask your deli to help you with other selections. **FRENCH CAMEMBERT,** one of the world's most renowned cheeses, can be substituted for any of the soft cheeses. Taste should be soft and delicate; if flavor is strong, it is past it's prime.

Domestic Boursin Cheese

6 ounces cream cheese, room temperature
1 stick of butter or butter substitute, room temperature
½ t. garlic powder

4 T. FRESHLY GRATED Parmesan cheese
2 T. dry white wine
2 T. minced fresh parsley
¼ t. thyme
¼ t. marjoram

1. In a mixing bowl, combine all ingredients. Blend in a food processor or mix an electric mixer until all ingredients are creamy and thoroughly mixed. See p. 42 "How to mince parsley easily."
2. Refrigerate at least two hours.
3. Butter hands to keep cheese from sticking. Remove from refrigerator and form into a ball. Sprinkle with paprika and serve with crackers.

Fruit to Accompany Cheeses

2-3 tart apples (Jonathan and Granny Smith) cut in wedges and leave unpeeled)

2 pounds seedless purple grapes

1. Cut apples into wedges, sprinkle with FRUIT FRESH (see p. 44), wrap in plastic wrap or put in airtight container and refrigerate until ready to use.
2. Wash and dry grapes. Cut into small clusters. Refrigerate until ready to serve.
3. Arrange cheeses attractively on board or tray with apples and clusters of grapes among the cheeses. Garnish with parsley.
4. Put Melba toast rounds and an assortment of crackers on each side of tray or board.

Assortment of Christmas Cookies and Candies

Choose from the treasury of Christmas Cookies, pages 167-174 and Christmas Candies, pages 189-195 and fill a shining tray with mouthwatering treats. Intersperse fresh holly leaves among the assortment.

Menu II

Sweet and Sour Meatballs

Savory Shrimp Mold

Garden Fresh Vegetable Tray

choice of

Five Minute Dip...

Curry Lover's Vegetable Dip...

Creamy Dill Dip

Zesty Onion Sandwiches

Fresh Apples Slices and Pear Wedges

served with

Chutney Bleu Cheese

Fruit Cake Slices

Assorted Cookies

Polynesian Sweet and Sour Meatballs

(make ahead—freezes well)
makes about 55 meatballs—allow
3 to 4 meatballs per person

Meat Balls

1½ lbs. LEAN ground beef	¼ t. garlic powder
¾ cup Old Fashioned Quaker Oats	¼ t. ginger
	1 t. Accent
1 8 oz. can sliced water chestnuts, drained and finely chopped	½ t. onion salt
	¼ t. salt
	¼ t. Tabasco
½ cup milk	1 T. Soy Sauce
1 egg, slightly beaten	

1. Mix all ingredients together well until thoroughly combined.
2. Form into balls about 1 inch to 1¼ inch.
3. When enough meat balls are ready for frying pan, brown first batch while continuing to make next amount.
4. Brown on medium low heat in a covered skillet, approximately 3 minutes on each side.
5. Drain well.

Continued on next page

Sauce

1 15½ oz. can crushed
  pineapple
1 7½ oz. can crushed
  pineapple, drained
1 firmly packed cup light
  brown sugar

1 cup beef bouillon
  (Swanson's preferred)
½ cup red wine vinegar
2 T. cornstarch
1 cup chopped green
  pepper (optional)

1. Drain 15½ oz. can crushed pineapple, reserving juice (should yield 1 cup).
2. Combine pineapple juice and brown sugar in 6 qt. pan.
3. Add bouillon and red wine vinegar.
4. Stir in 2 T. cornstarch and whisk until thoroughly dissolved.
5. Bring to rolling boil, reduce heat, and cook until slightly thickened, stirring constantly (approximately 8 minutes).
6. Drain 7½ oz. can pineapple.
7. Add both cans drained pineapple, green pepper, and meat balls.
8. Simmer in sauce until thoroughly heated through— approximately 10-12 minutes.
9. Transfer to chafing dish or heated bowl.

   (Furnish guests with toothpicks for spearing meat balls)

Savory Shrimp Mold

(see rule for congealed salads, p. 230)
Freezes well
Serves 10-12 (or 30 if spread on crackers)

1 lb. cooked, peeled, and deveined shrimp
3 envelopes plain gelatin
1 14½ oz. can Swanson's Chicken Broth
1 10¾ oz. can Cream of Shrimp soup
1 8 oz. package cream cheese, softened
½ t. Tabasco
3 T. bottled lemon juice or 4 T. fresh lemon juice — taste — add more if desired
½ t. salt
1 green onion chopped in 4 pieces
1 8 oz. carton sour cream
1 cup celery, chopped fine
olives, pimento, and parsley for garnish

1. Chop coarsely one half of the shrimp (¼ to ½ inches each piece). Set aside.
2. Pour one half can of Chicken Broth into saucepan and heat on medium high.
3. Sprinkle gelatin on remainder of Chicken Broth in can to soften.
4. Add gelatin mixture to hot Chicken Broth, stir until dissolved, and remove from heat.
5. Place in blender: remainder of shrimp (unchopped), shrimp soup, cream cheese, Tabasco, lemon juice, salt, green onion, and Chicken Broth gelatin mixture.
6. Blend on high until all ingredients are thoroughly combined, pouring half of mixture into mixing bowl.
7. Add sour cream to mixture in blender. Blend and pour into mixing bowl with other half of blended mousse.
8. Stir until well combined.
9. Fold in chopped celery and chopped shrimp.
10. Pour mixture into lightly oiled 1½ qt. mold, round bowl, or fish mold.
11. Cover and refrigerate until firm.
12. Unmold on round platter, surround with crackers, and garnish with olives, pimento strips, and parsley.

Garden Fresh Vegetable Tray

(prepare the day before…choose at least four of the following)
4 or 5 choices will serve 18-20

1 head cauliflower, separated into flowerettes
1 bunch brocooli, flowerettes only
½ lb. button mushrooms
2 green peppers, cut into thin strips
1 small bunch carrots, cut into sticks

1 pint cherry tomatoes, stemmed
2 medium sized zucchini, thinly sliced
1 bunch celery, cut into sticks
Parsley for garnish

1. Wash all vegetables and drain well.
2. Separate cauliflower and broccoli into flowerettes.
3. Cut green peppers into strips.
4. Clean carrots and celery and cut into sticks.
5. Stem tomatoes and mushrooms.
6. Store in airtight containers in refrigerator until ready to use.
7. At serving time, cluster vegetables on an attractive tray, placing glass bowl of dip in center. Garnish liberally with parsley.

CHOOSE ONE OF THE FOLLOWING DIPS OR SERVE ALL THREE

A Different Twist

Instead of a crystal or glass serving bowl, buy a large red cabbage, hollow out, fluff outside leaves, and spoon dip into center just before serving. Surround with vegetables for dipping and garnish liberally with parsley. (See page 42 for illustration.)

Five Minute Dip

Makes 2 cups — keeps for a week to 10 days

1 8 oz. package cream cheese, softened
1 cup mayonnaise (no substitutes except "lite" mayonnaise)

1 1-oz. package Hidden Valley Ranch Salad Dressing Mix

1 Combine all ingredients and mix well with fork until thoroughly blended.
2. Place in serving dish, cover, and refrigerate until ready to use.
3. At serving time sprinkle lightly with paprika and surround with fresh vegetables.

Curry Lover's Vegetable Dip

Make ahead — keeps well for a week to 10 days
Makes 1½ cups

1 cup mayonnaise or "lite" mayonnaise
½ cup sour cream or "lite sour cream"
1 t. curry powder

½ t. paprika
½ t. dry mustard
¼ t. Tabasco
1 t. fresh lemon juice

1. Put all ingredients in a medium size mixing bowl.
2. Whisk until well blended.
3. Cover and refrigerate until ready to serve. At serving time, sprinkle lightly with paprika for color.

Creamy Dill

Make ahead—keeps well refrigerated for 1 week to 10 days
Makes 2½ cups

1 cup sour cream or "lite sour cream"
1 cup mayonnaise or "lite" mayonnaise
4 T. finely chopped parsley*
4 T. finely chopped green onions, tops also

1 T. dill weed (more if strong dill flavor preferred)
¼ t. salt
2 t. Worcestershire sauce
1 T. plus 1 t. fresh lemon juice

1. In a medium size mixing bowl, combine all ingredients.
2. Whisk until well blended.
3. Cover and refrigerate until ready to serve. At serving time, sprinkle lightly with paprika for color.

*AN EASY METHOD TO CHOP PARSLEY: Put parsley in a mug or 8 ounce glass. Snip with scissors until finely chopped.

Zesty Onion Sandwiches

A real crowd pleaser—They disappear in a hurry!
Makes 30 finger size sandwiches (allow 3-4 per person)

**1 pound red onions
(approximately 2 medium
large onions)
½ t. salt for ice water
1 loaf very thin sliced, *fairly
dry*, white bread
(Earthgrains, Arnold, or
Pepperidge Farm
preferred)**

**2 T. mayonnaise or "lite"
mayonnaise
¼ t. salt
¼ t. pepper, coarsely
ground**

DAY BEFORE:

1. Chop onions finely, removing and discarding hard core in center.
2. Place in small bowl, add ½ t. salt, cover with ice water and plastic wrap.
3. Place in refrigerator overnight.
4. Cut crusts from as many bread slices as needed. Two slices will make four sandwiches.
5. Cover bread tightly with foil, plastic wrap, or put in ziploc bags. Refrigerate until ready to spread.

DAY OF PARTY:*

1. Drain onions well. Pat with paper towels until all moisture is absorbed.
2. Mix chopped onions with 2 T. mayonnaise, and ¼ t. each salt and pepper. Taste—add 1 t. more mayonnaise if needed. Cover and refrigerate until ready to spread.
3. Lightly spread each slice of bread with mayonnaise.
4. Spoon 2 T. onion mixture on one half of bread slices. Top with remaining bread and cut each sandwich into fourths.*
5. Place on a cookie sheet, wrap tightly, and refrigerate until ready to serve.
6. At serving time, place on a glass platter or silver tray, sprinkle lightly with paprika and garnish with parsley.

   *Sandwiches can be made 4-5 hours before the party.

Fresh Apple Slices and Pear Wedges

Prepare early in the day and cover with Fruit Fresh)

2-3 tart red and green apples   **2-3 ripe pears**

1. Cut apples into thin wedges. Each apple should yield about 18-20 wedges. Leave skin on for color and ease of handling.
2. Cut pears into wedges—depending on size, each pear should yield 12-15 wedges. Do not peel.
3. Sprinkle with Fruit Fresh (See directions below) and put in two separate containers. Cover tightly and refrigerate until ready to serve.
4. At serving time, drain any liquid off, pat dry, and arrange attractively on a serving platter. Garnish with parsley or fresh holly and serve with Chutney and a wedge of Blue Cheese.

Fruit Fresh

(for preserving fresh fruit)
Makes enough for 4 cups fruit

2 t. Fruit Fresh   **3 T. water**

1. Dissolve Fruit Fresh in water and toss with fruit.
2. Wrap tightly in plastic wrap or put in airtight container and refrigerate until ready to use.

Chutney Blue Cheese

(Blue cheese and chutney are tasty accompaniments to pears and apples)

1 6-8 ounce wedge blue cheese
Unseasoned crackers or Melba Toast rounds

1 8½ ounce jar chutney (Major Grey's available nationwide)

1. In center of platter, place wedge of blue cheese and a small bowl of chutney.
2. Surround attractively with pear and apple wedges.
3. Place crackers to the side.
4. Guests can dip fruit into the chutney if desired or place chutney on top of a bite of blue cheese along with a nibble of apple and pear.

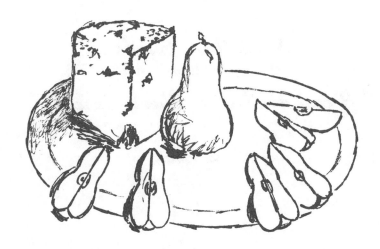

Dessert

Prepare early in the day and cover tightly with plastic wrap. Take your choice of the variety of Christmas cookies offered, pages 167-174. Plan ahead and freeze. Slice Fruit Cake p. 175, in thin, bite sized pieces. Arrange attractively on a large platter, garnish with fresh holly if available, and place on buffet or serving table.

Menu III

Carolina Cheese Biscuits

Succulent Assorted Cold Cuts

Potato Rolls and Party Rye

Scalloped Crab

with

Melba Toast Rounds

Cocoanut Chutney Cheese Spread

Fruit Bowl

of

Green Cherry Pineapple Spears

and

Frosted Grapes

Carolina Cheese Biscuits

An old family favorite
(Make ahead—freezes well)
Makes 42 biscuits

2 sticks butter (or butter substitute), room temperature
2 cups grated SHARP cheddar cheese, room temperature

2 cups pre sifted flour
¼ t. salt
⅛ t. tabasco
paprika
pecan halves (optional)

1. Preheat oven to 350 degrees.
2. Mix together butter, cheese, flour, salt, and tabasco either by hand or with an electric mixer until all ingredients are well blended.
3. Lightly flour rolling pin and counter.
4. Roll out dough to ⅜ inch thickness.
5. Cut in round 1¾ inches in diameter.

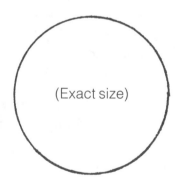

(Exact size)

6. Sprinkle lightly with paprika and place pecan half in center if desired.
7. Place on a lightly greased cookie sheet and bake 18-20 minutes or until light golden brown.
8. Remove from cookie sheet, let cool, and store in airtight tin or ziploc bag until ready to use.
9. Reheat in a 200 degree oven for 10-12 minutes to crisp up if frozen.

Succulent Assorted Cold Cuts

For convenience, buy from the deli
Choose at least 2 or more meats, allowing ⅛ lb. meat per
person, per sandwich.

Corned beef, thinly sliced
Rare roast of beef,
thinly sliced
Ham, thinly sliced
Smoked turkey,
thinly sliced

1 head curly endive or fresh
parsley
Potato rolls
(allow 2 per person)
1-2 loaves Party rye bread

1. On large serving tray arrange meat attractively. Garnish with curly endive or parsley.
2. Place potato rolls and rye bread in bread trays or baskets beside serving tray.
3. Serve with choice of mayonnaise and mustard mayonnaise.

Mustard Mayonnaise

Preparation time: 7 minutes
Makes 2 cups

3 T. dry mustard
2 T. cider vinegar
⅛ t. Tabasco

½ t. horseradish
2 cups mayonnaise
(no substitutes)

1. Dissolve mustard in vinegar.
2. Add Tabasco and horseradish.
3. Blend in mayonnaise and mix well.

Scalloped Crab

Serves 15-18

1 pound fresh (if possible)
   select crab meat
4 T. butter (½ stick) or
   butter substitute
4 T. All Purpose flour
2 cups whole milk
2 cups grated Swiss cheese
   (better if bought in bulk
   and grated at home)

1 egg yolk, beaten
½ t. Worcestershire Sauce
¼ t. Tabasco
¼ t. salt
¼ scant t. black pepper
3 T. lemon juice
2 T. dry sherry
½ cup sour cream
White Melba toast rounds

1. Go through crab meat and carefully remove any shells. Refrigerate until ready to use.
2. In a 2 quart saucepan, melt butter on medium heat. Add flour and stir until well blended.
3. Add milk, stirring until blended and thickened slightly.
4. Add grated Swiss cheese and beaten egg yolk, mixing well.
5. Stir occasionally until cheese has melted.
6. Add Worcestershire sauce, Tabasco, salt, pepper, lemon juice and sherry.
7. Stir in sour cream, mixing well. Put cover on pan and set aside or refrigerate until ready to add crab.
8. Lastly, add crab, heating on lowest heat until mixture is heated throughout.
9. Pour in chafing dish over hot water or in a heated serving dish on an electric hot plate. Sprinkle lightly with paprika for color and garnish with parsley.
10. Surround with Melba toast and serve.

Cocoanut Chutney Cheese Spread

Freezes well—keeps frozen up to three months
Serves 60-70 on bite size crackers
Makes 2 8″ molds

24 ounces regular or "lite" cream cheese, room temperature
1 cup sour cream or "lite" sour cream
8 slices cooked and crumbled bacon
½ cup finely chopped green onion tops

2 t. curry powder
1 cup chopped raisins
1 cup salted and chopped peanuts (measure 1 cup peanuts first, then chop)
2 8-inch aluminum foil pie tins

TOPPING

1 8 ounce jar chutney (Major Grey's available in all grocery stores)
1 cup flaked cocoanut
parsley for garnish

1. Chop 1 cup peanuts either in Cuisnart or put in ziploc bag, close tightly, and hammer until finely chopped. Set aside.
2. Chop coarsely one cup raisins with a chopping knife. Set aside.
3. Combine cream cheese, sour cream, crumbled bacon, chopped green onion, and curry powder. Mix until all ingredients are well blended.
4. Fold in chopped raisins and chopped peanuts.
5. Lightly grease or spray with a "no stick cooking spray" 2 8-inch aluminum foil pie tins.
6. Press cheese mixture into the two pie tins, wrap well with plastic wrap, then freezer paper. Place in freezer until ready to use. If using immediately, place in freezer until hard, then unmold.
7. To unmold: Bend sides of pie tins up, flip out on serving platter. Spread chutney evenly over tops and sides. Sprinkle all over with ½ cup cocoanut per mold. Garnish lavishly with parsley.

Continued on next page

8. Serve with assorted crackers to the side.

   *This mold will take about 2 hours to thaw out at room temperature.

Green Cherry Pineapple Spears and Frosted Grapes

Serves 10-12

GREEN CHERRY PINEAPPLE SPEARS

1 20 oz. can of pineapple chunks, drained or equal amount of fresh pineapple

2 small bottles green Maraschino cherries
2½ T. light rum
Festive toothpicks

1. Drain pineapple and cherries, patting dry with paper towel.
2. Put in mixing bowl, toss with 2½ T. light rum. Cover and refrigerate for 2-3 hours.
3. Before serving drain rum from pineapple and cherries.
4. On festive toothpicks alternate 2 pineapple chunks and 1 cherry until all have been used.
5. Arrange on serving platter with frosted grapes, cover with plastic wrap, and refrigerate until party time.

FROSTED GRAPES

1-2 pounds purple seedless grapes

4 egg whites
granulated sugar

1. Cut grapes in small clusters—no more than 5-6 per bunch.
2. Beat egg whites with wire whisk until frothy.
3. Dip and coat with egg whites.
4. Sprinkle with sugar until evenly coated.
5. Place on waxed paper in refrigerator to harden.
6. Mound in bowl or on platter with Green Cherry Pineapple Spears.

ALL ABOARD! HERE COMES THE KINDERGARTEN BUNCH!

All Aboard! Here Comes The Kindergarten Bunch!

There is an unforgettable light in a child's eye when Christmas approaches. What fun to share their excitement, but remember a few rules before issuing invitations.

A large number of children can be uncontrollable. Limit guests to six or less. Six children will seem like a large, lively group and four will be a party.

Do not let the party last too long—children tire easily and attention spans are short at this age.

Never surprise your child with a party—anticipation is half the fun.

Most importantly—HAVE FUN, both young and old!

Menu I .... p. 55
"SNOWMAN SPECIAL"
Snowmen Sandwiches
Carrot Sticks
Potato Chips
Punch
Ice Cream Bars
Puddin' Paintings

Menu II .... p. 59
"RUDOLPH'S PARTY"
Animals To Eat
Serendipity Salad
Potato Chips
Punch
Kindergartener's Own Cup Cakes

Menu III... p. 64
"SANTA'S SNACK"
or
(When A Mother Feels Brave!)
Peanut Butter and Jelly Sandwiches
Upside Down Pears
Potato Chips
Punch
Ticky-Tacky Taffy

Menu I

"SNOWMAN SPECIAL"

Snowman Sandwiches

Carrot Sticks

Potato Chips

Christmas Punch

Ice Cream Bars

Fun and Games

Puddin' Paintings

Who Put The Carrot In The Snowman's Nose?

Snowman Sandwiches

Bread slices cut out in shape of snowmen and other related Christmas figures

8 ounce package cream cheese, softened

3 T. mayonnaise

In Individual Bowls:

raisins (for eyes)
pimiento strips (for mouth)
sliced rounds of bananas (beard)
celery leaves (hair)
celery strips & carrot strips (pipe)

small squares carrots (pipe bowl)
sprigs of parsley (hair)
carrots or celery diced (buttons)

1. Have bread slices already cut out. These may be done ahead of time and frozen.
2. Combine cream cheese and mayonnaise and whisk until creamy. Set aside in bowl.
3. On kitchen table place cream cheese mixture, bread cut outs, and all accompaniments.
4. Help children spread cream cheese on bread. Let them decorate snowmen sandwiches according to their imagination. Serve carrot sticks, potato chips, and punch along with sandwiches.

Option: Cut bread in triangles for Christmas tree—spread with cream cheese and decorate with parsley, pimiento, carrots.

Christmas Punch

(Inexpensive, tasty and nutritious — can be made ahead or frozen)
Serves 25-30

4 cups cranberry juice   **2 cups lemonade**
4 cups orange juice   **2 quarts gingerale***

1. Combine cranberry juice, orange juice, and lemonade. Stir to mix well.
2. Just before serving, add gingerale and serve ice cold.
   ***If freezing, add gingerale just before serving.**

Ice Cream Bars

Buy ice cream bars and have in freezer for dessert. Supply extra napkins for dribbles.

"Fun and Games"

Puddin' Paintings

(Prepare pudding day before)

1. Buy several boxes (different flavors) instant pudding mix.
2. Add a few drops of red or green food coloring to vanilla pudding if desired.
3. Spread newspapers or a plastic cloth to cover kitchen table.
4. Have puddings already mixed up in separate bowls placed on table.
5. Give each child a piece of white paper large enough to paint on.
6. Children dip their fingers into the various puddings and come up with their own paintings. Licking excess pudding off their fingers gives them a second dessert!

Who Put The Carrot in the Snowman's Nose?

1. Draw a snowman's head on poster board; cut a hole for the nose.
2. Prop board on an easel or in front of a large box.
3. Blindfold each child and give him a carrot to drop through the nose.
4. A prize can be given to the child who drops the carrot through the hole.

Menu II

"RUDOLPH'S PARTY"

Animals To Eat

Serendipity Salad

Potato Chips

Punch

Kindergartener's Own Cup Cakes

Fun and Games

Pin The Nose On Rudolph

Surprise Christmas Package

Animals To Eat

Children are fascinated with sandwiches served in unusual
shapes

**Bread slices already cut out
in various animal
shapes—rabbit, reindeer,
cat, dog,
lion, etc.**

**8 ounces cream cheese,
softened**
3 T. mayonnaise

In Individual Bowls:

raisins (eyes)
diced carrots (nose)
sliced bananas (cheeks)
**celery strips (ears) and
celery leaves (hair)**

**crushed pineapple, drained
(lion's mane)**
pimiento strips (mouth)
sprigs of parsley (fur)

1. Have animal shapes already cut out. These can be done
   ahead and frozen.
2. Combine cream cheese and mayonnaise and whisk until
   creamy. Set aside in bowl.
3. On kitchen table place cream cheese, animal cut outs and
   all accompaniments.
4. Let children choose which animals they want to decorate
   and eat.
5. Help them spread cream cheese on cut outs, then let their
   imagination run wild.
6. Serve sandwiches with Serendipity Salad, potato chips,
   and punch, p. 57.

Serendipity Salad

Colorful and nutritious
Make ahead

1 6 ounce package strawberry or raspberry jello
2 cups boiling water
1 cup cold water

1 16 ounce can fruit cocktail, drained
1 banana, cut into small chunks
1 cup miniature marshmallows

1. In a mixing bowl, dissolve jello in 2 cups boiling water. Stir to mix well. Add 1 cup cold water and stir.
2. Refrigerate until partially set or put in freezer until it begins to set up.
3. Fold in fruit cocktail, banana, and marshmallows.
4. Refrigerate until set.
5. When set, spoon into clear plastic glasses (6 ounce), cover with plastic wrap, and refrigerate until ready to serve.

Kindergartener's Own Cupcakes

Make ahead and freeze—have ready for children
to decorate
Makes 24-28 cupcakes

**1 18 ounce package white
or yellow cake mix (Betty
Crocker, Duncan Hines,
or Pillsbury Super Moist)**

**1 cup water
½ cup vegetable oil
3 eggs**

1. Preheat oven to 350 degrees.
2. In a mixing bowl, blend cake mix, water, oil, and eggs. Beat until well mixed.
3. Spoon into paper liners in a cupcake pan. Fill only ⅔ full.
4. Bake 22-27 minutes or until golden brown and cupcake springs back when touched lighty in center.
5. Cool and store in airtight container or freeze until ready to ice and decorate.

TOPPING

**White icing in mix or can
Cinnamon candies
Silver dragees (Betty
    Crocker in a 2 ounce jar)
Rainbow mix (Betty
    Crocker in a 2 ounce jar)
Cocoanut
Food coloring**

**Chocolate chips
Gum drops or jelly beans
Miniature marshmallows
Red licorice (cut in strips)
Crushed pineapple, drained
Maraschino cherries,
    drained**

1. Spread newspapers or a plastic cloth over kitchen table.
2. Have all decorations on table.
3. Color individual bowls of cocoanut with food coloring for hair.
4. Help children spread icing over cupcake top.
5. Let them help themselves to the assortment of decorations offered to make happy faces on the cupcakes. Ample number of cupcakes to eat for dessert and take a few home to show off their art work!

"Fun and Games"

Pin The Nose On Rudolph

1. Draw and color "Rudolph the Red Nosed Reindeer" on poster board. Leave off nose. Or buy a large cut out of Rudolph and cut off nose.
2. Draw and paint separately a large red nose.
3. Pin reindeer up on a wall.
4. Blindfold each child and let him see if he can pin the nose on Rudolph.
5. A prize can be given to the child coming the closest (optional).

Surprise Christmas Package

1. Giftwrap a prize in a small box.
2. Place the wrapped box in a slightly larger box and wrap it.
3. Repeat 6 or 7 times until you have a nest of boxes, each gift wrapped.
4. Place children in a circle on the floor.
5. As Christmas music plays, have them pass the large box around the circle. Stop the music and the child holding the package must unwrap it.
6. This is repeated until the smallest box is left. The child who opens it wins the prize.

"SANTA'S SNACK"

or

(When A Mother Feels Brave!)

Peanut Butter and Jelly Sandwiches

Upside Down Pears

Potato Chips

Punch

Ticky-Tacky Taffy

Peanut Butter and Jelly Sandwiches

(Children are fascinated with sandwiches served in unusual shapes)
Cut bread shapes out several weeks ahead and freeze

Bread slices cut in rounds, triangles, Christmas trees, Santa's stars, etc.

Peanut butter
Jelly

1. Spread peanut butter and jelly on a bread cut out and top with another slice of the identical shape.
2. Can be made early in the day and covered with aluminum foil or a slightly dampened dish towel.
3. Serve with potato chips, Upside Down Pears, and punch, p. 57.

Upside Down Pears

Make early in the day, cover, and refrigerate

1 16 ounce can pear halves, drained (can also use peaches)
cottage cheese
maraschino cherries

raisins
parsley or curly celery leaves
toothpicks

1. Drain peaches and pat dry with a paper towel.
2. Place a small dab of cottage cheese on a lettuce leaf. Cover with a peach or pear turned upside down.
3. Secure two cherries with toothpick for eyes, dot raisins in for nose, and cut cherries in half or thinly slice a piece of orange rind for the mouth.
4. Use toothpick to hold if needed.
5. Your artistic endeavors may not look like the work of the great masters, but be assured children will love them.

Ticky-Tacky Taffy

Only to be made when a mother feels brave!

or

Refer to Fun and Games in Menus I and II for
other suggestions

1¼ cups sugar   **¼ cup water**
1½ t. margarine   **½ t. vanilla**
2 T. mild vinegar

1. Heavily grease a marble slab or kitchen counter with margarine.
2. In a 2 quart saucepan, put sugar, margarine, vinegar, and water.
3. Cook quickly, stirring, until a small bit dropped in a cup of cold water forms a hard ball (265 degrees on the candy thermometer). **Do not let children near hot syrup.**
4. Stir in vanilla.
5. Pour this sticky mess onto buttered slab. Hold pouring edge of pan away from you and only a few inches above counter so you won't get splattered. Let cool until a dent can be made in it when pressed with a finger.
6. When cool enough to handle, pick it up (have hands buttered) and make into a ball.
7. Have children butter their hands.
8. Everyone pull, and pull, and pull! Taffy will turn light brown in color and elastic. When it does, stretch what isn't in the floor into a long thin rope about 1 inch thick. The pulling process may take anywhere from 5 to 20 minutes depending upon weather conditions and ability of "pullers."
9. Put rope on counter, cut with well buttered scissors into desired sizes, and let each child wrap a certain amount to take home for Santa's snack!

ONCE AGAIN THAT WONDROUS CHRISTMAS FEAST

The Richly Flavored Traditional

The Classic Victorian

The Sumptuous Buffet

ONCE AGAIN THAT WONDROUS CHRISTMAS FEAST

"THE RICHLY FLAVORED TRADITIONAL"

Tray of Celery and Stuffed Olives
Golden Roast Turkey with Herbed Cornbread Dressing
Giblet Gravy
Plantation Brandied Sweet Potatoes
Chesapeake Bay Scalloped Oysters
English Peas in Consommé
New England Cranberry Conserve
Piquant Pineapple Almond Salad
Ambrosia

"THE CLASSIC VICTORIAN"

Tray of Celery and Stuffed Olives
Succulent Roast Duckling with Fruit Stuffing
Orange Sauce
French Green Beans with Slivered Almonds
Steamed Wild Rice
Cranberry Salad
English Plum Pudding
with
Peach Brandy Sauce

"THE SUMPTUOUS BUFFET"

Tray of Celery and Stuffed Olives
Glazed, Spiral-Sliced, Ready to Serve Ham
Mustard Sauce
Roast Turkey Supreme
Herbed Cornbread Dressing Balls
Giblet Gravy
Jellied Cranberry Sauce
Artichoke and Spinach Casserole
Christmas Ribbon Salad
Fruit Cake Slices

All About Turkey

CHOOSING YOUR TURKEY

1. With modern feeding methods, most turkeys on the market need not be over six months old. Hens and Toms are about the same in tenderness. You DO NOT need to pay more for a hen.
2. Look for plump white birds, well rounded over the breast bone. A fresh turkey is always preferable, but modern freezing methods produce excellent birds.

HOW LARGE A TURKEY TO BUY?

1. If you expect to serve turkey for more than one meal, allow at least 1½ to 2 pounds per person.
2. Serving for one meal only:
   Allow ¾ to 1 pound per person if turkey weighs LESS than 12 pounds.
   Allow ½ to ¾ pound per serving for turkeys weighing OVER 12 pounds.

THAWING THE TURKEY

LEAVE IN THE ORIGINAL WRAP FOR ALL THREE METHODS OF THAWING — THIS WILL KEEP JUICE LOSS TO A MINIMUM.

METHOD I
Place on a tray in refrigerator in original wrap.
Allow: 3 days for defrosting a 10-14 pound turkey
4 days for defrosting a 15-20 pound turkey

METHOD II
Leave in original wrap. Cover with cold water, changing water every hour.

WEIGHT	APPROXIMATE THAWING TIME
10-12 pounds	5-6 hours
12-14 pounds	6-7 hours
14-16 pounds	7-8 hours
16-18 pounds	8-9 hours
18-20 pounds	9-10 hours

METHOD III
MICROWAVE METHOD — POWER LEVEL DEFROST
Allow 9-11 minutes per pound

1. Leave turkey in original wrap.
2. Place bird breast side down in oven with legs pointing to right in oven.
3. Microwave at DEFROST for half of the defrosting time.

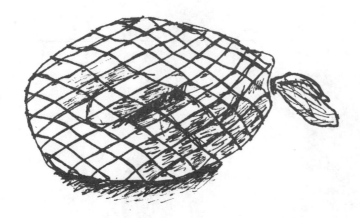

Continued on next page

4. Unwrap turkey. Shield with foil, legs, wing tips, breast, tail, any area that appears to be warm to the touch of your fingers. Secure foil with toothpicks.

5. Place turkey, breast side up, with legs pointing to the left of oven. Defrost for second half of time.

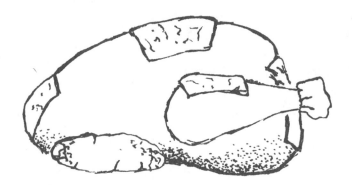

6. Remove metal clamp from legs. Run cold water into breast and neck cavities until giblets and neck can be removed. Turkey should feel soft and cool with a glistening surface and interior should be cold to slightly icy. Refrigerate until ready to cook.

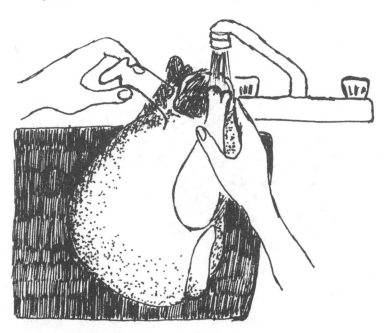

Menu 1

Tray of Celery and Stuffed Olives

Golden Roast Turkey

Herbed Cornbread Dressing

Giblet Gravy

Plantation Brandied Sweet Potatoes

Chesapeake Bay Scalloped Oysters

English Peas in Consomme

Deliciously Different Cranberry Conserve

Piquant Pineapple Almond Salad

Hot Rolls

Ambrosia

Choice of Red and White Wine

Coffee

Golden Roast Turkey

(Read "All About Turkey" p. 70 before cooking
your turkey)

TIMETABLE FOR ROASTING UNSTUFFED TURKEY

Weight of unstuffed, ready-to-cook turkey (pounds)	Cooking time for foil-tent method, at 325°F (hours)
6 to 8	2¼ to 3¼
8 to 12	3 to 4
12 to 16	3½ to 4½
16 to 20	4 to 5
20 to 24	4½ to 5½

Turkey is done when meat thermometer in thigh registers 180 to 185°F, or breast temperature registers 170 to 175°F and leg joint moves freely.

TIMETABLE FOR ROASTING STUFFED TURKEY

Weight of unstuffed, ready-to-cook turkey (pounds)	Cooking time for foil-tent method, at 325°F (hours)
6 to 8	3 to 3½
8 to 12	3½ to 4½
12 to 16	4½ to 5½
16 to 20	5½ to 6½
20 to 24	6½ to 7

Turkey is done when meat thermometer in thigh registers 180 to 185°F, or breast temperature registers 170 to 175°F and leg joint moves freely.

Golden Roast Turkey

1. Preheat oven to 450 degrees.
2. Remove giblets and neck from cavities and set aside.
3. Rinse outside and cavities of bird with cold water. Pat dry.
4. Fill neck and body cavities lightly with stuffing. (See p. 78 for recipe.) DO NOT CRAM IN STUFFING–it will expand during cooking. Reserve rest of stuffing to be cooked separately. (NOTE–if you do not wish to stuff the turkey, follow directions below.)
5. Fasten skin of neck and body cavities with metal skewers. If you do not have skewers, sew with a heavy thread, pin with large safety pins, or use unbent paper clips as fasteners.
6. Cross drumsticks and tie drumsticks to tail with a soft string–this keeps dressing in place.
7. Rub entire bird with butter (or butter substitute) and lightly salt (optional) and pepper all over.
8. Place bird in roaster breast side up.
9. Cover bottom of pan with water–approximately ½ to 1 cup water. Add 1-2 stalks of celery and ½ peeled white onion. If turkey is unstuffed, lay celery and onion inside cavity. (This flavors the drippings for the gravy).
10. Put lid on or cover loosely with a tent of aluminum foil.
11. Place in a preheated 450 degree oven. IMMEDIATELY REDUCE HEAT TO 325 DEGREES.
12. Follow the cooking time chart on p.74.
13. Baste occasionally with drippings while turkey is cooking.

NOTE: If you do not want to go to the trouble of stuffing your bird, put all dressing in a lightly greased casserole (or spray baking dish with a "no stick baking spray") and cook 1-1½ hours at 325 degrees. It is important to baste with turkey dripping occasionally to give dressing a moist consistency and a good flavor.

Continued on next page

FINISHING THE TURKEY

1. 30 to 40 minutes before time table indicates turkey will be done, remove lid or aluminum foil, baste with juices or rub with butter, and allow for final browning.
2. At this time, also test for doneness. Meat thermometer will register 185 degrees when placed in the thigh muscle. OR, if not using a meat thermometer, move the drum stick up and down. If done, the joint should give readily or break. The breast meat will be very soft when pressed between the fingers.

WHAT TO DO IF TURKEY IS DONE, BUT NOT BROWN?

Run under the broiler until golden brown and remove to serving platter.

WHAT TO DO IF TURKEY HAS BROWNED, BUT IS NOT DONE?

Put lid or aluminum foil tent back on roaster and continue cooking until it tests done.

PRESENTATION

1. Lift Turkey onto serving platter. Place breast side up.
2. Cover with foil and let stand 20 minutes. This will let the juices be absorbed into the meat and make carving easier.
3. Garnish with parsley when ready to serve.

CARVING THE TURKEY
...YOU WILL NEED...

A Sharp Carving Knife and a Two to Four Tinned Meat Fork
An extra serving plate to place sliced meat

1. Insert fork firmly into drum stick joint, pulling the leg away from body of bird. Slice down until the ball and socket hip joint is exposed. To sever, make a twisting motion with the knife and continue to hold down firmly with the fork. Then cut joint as shown.

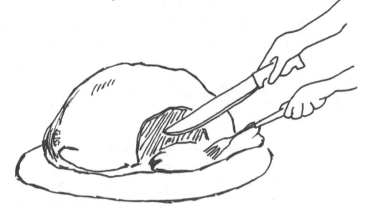

Repeat the above, cutting off other leg. Some slices of meat may be cut from the thigh and drumstick at this point and set aside for those who prefer dark meat.

2. Proceed to remove wings in a similar manner to above instructions.

3. To slice the breast, begin at area nearest the neck and slice thinly across the grain. Slice entire length of breast. Carve only one side until more is needed for a second helping.

Herbed Cornbread Dressing

Makes 9-10 cups—enough to stuff a 14-16 pound turkey
with extra left over for a separate casserole

STUFFING DO'S AND DON'TS

1. Stuffing can be made the day before. Store in refrigerator in covered dish. Remove 20 to 30 minutes prior to cooking. DO NOT STUFF TURKEY UNTIL READY TO COOK.
2. Handle stuffing lightly so it will not compact.
3. Do not cram stuffing in turkey cavities—it will expand during cooking.
4. Cook extra stuffing in a greased baking dish.

Dressing

1 8 ounce bag Pepperidge Farm Herb Seasoned Stuffing
1 8 ounce bag Pepperidge Farm Cornbread Stuffing
2 cups hot water
2 sticks butter or butter substitute
2 beaten eggs

1 cup chopped onion
1 cup chopped celery
½ cup chopped parsley or 1 T. dried parsley
1 t. dried sage
¼ t. salt (or more to taste)
½ t. coarsely ground black pepper

1. Bring 2 cups water to boil. Add butter, reduce heat, and let butter melt.
2. In a large mixing bowl, combine Herb Stuffing, Cornbread Stuffing, two beaten eggs, chopped onion, chopped celery, parsley, sage, salt, and pepper. Toss lightly to mix well.
3. Add melted butter/water combination and stir lightly until well blended.
4. Stuff turkey according to directions on p. 75. Place extra dressing in greased and covered baking dish. Cook for 40 minutes at 325 degrees while turkey is finishing. Baste extra dressing occasionally with turkey drippings.

Giblet Gravy

Makes 7 cups
Allow ½ cup per person

Reserved giblets and neck
of turkey
1 celery stalk
½ white onion

1 t. salt
1½ t. black pepper
water to cover

• • • • • • • • • • •

6 T. flour
drippings from turkey

salt and pepper

1. While turkey is roasting, place giblets, neck, celery, onion, salt and pepper in a 3 quart saucepan. Cover with water.
2. Bring to a boil. Reduce heat to a low simmer. Cover and cook for 2 hours. Check water level from time to time and add more water if necessary to keep giblets covered.
3. Remove from heat, drain, reserving broth and giblets. Set aside. Discard neck, onion, and celery.
4. Coarsely chop giblets and set aside.
5. When turkey is done, remove to heated platter.
6. Pour pan drippings into a bowl and let stand a few minutes until fat separates from meat juices.
7. Skim 6 T. fat from drippings into sauce pan. Blend in 6 T. flour and stir with whisk on medium high heat until flour has thickened and mixture is well combined and smooth. Reduce heat to medium low.
8. Add reserved broth and "defatted" drippings, and enough water to make 7 cups. Continue to cook slowly, stirring, until gravy is medium consistency. If a thicker gravy is desired, decrease liquid to 6 cups.
9. Add chopped giblets and taste. Add salt and pepper if needed.
10. Remove from stove and reheat when ready to serve.

Plantation Brandied Sweet Potatoes

TO PREPARE COOKED SWEET POTATOES
Conventional Method

1. Drop unpeeled sweet potatoes in boiling water.
2. Cover, reduce heat to a medium boil, and cook approximately 35-40 minutes until just tender. When pierced with a fork, middle of potato should feel tender, but slightly resistent to fork.
3. Let cool partially before peeling.

Microwave Method

1. Pierce potatoes all over with a cooking fork to release steam when cooking.
2. Place potatoes on a paper towel on shelf of oven in a star position about 1 inch apart.

3. Follow cooking guide below: Cook on high power. Chart is for potatoes weighing 6 to 8 ounces. Cooking temperature—HIGH. Turn potatoes over when one half cooking time is completed.

1 potato	4-6 minutes
2 potatoes	6-8 minutes
4 potatoes	12-16 minutes
6 potatoes	20-24 minutes
8 potatoes	28-32 minutes

IMPORTANT—Potatoes will feel firm when done. If left standing 5 minutes, they will continue to cook and soften. For the following recipe, cook potatoes only until just tender and run under cold water to stop cooking process.

Plantation Brandied Sweet Potatoes

Make ahead and freeze–wrap casserole dish tightly in plastic wrap or aluminum foil, then in freezer wrap.

Serves 8

6 medium sized baked sweet potatoes– (approximately 5 to 5½ pounds)
1 cup brown sugar, firmly packed
½ t. cinnamon
½ t. nutmeg

½ t. Pumpkin Pie Spice
¼ t. salt
1 cup English walnuts (or pecans), broken up
¾ cup brandy (Sherry can be substituted)
6 T. butter (¾ stick) or butter substitute

1. Preheat oven to 375 degrees.*
1. Peel baked sweet potatoes. Slice one half inch thick then cut into serving pieces if too large.
2. Combine brown sugar, cinnamon, nutmeg, Pumpkin Pie Spice, salt and nuts. Stir to mix well.
3. Sprinkle mixture evenly over potatoes.
4. Pour brandy over all.
5. Dot with 6 T. butter broken into small pieces.
6. Cover and bake 30 minutes at 375 degrees. Baste occasionally.

*If cooking in same oven with turkey, bake 325 degrees for 1 hour to 1 hour 20 minutes, basting occasionally and cooking until most of juices are absorbed.

Chesapeake Bay Scalloped Oysters

Deliciously easy!
Keep oysters packed in crushed ice and covered in
refrigerator until ready to use–do not freeze
Serves 6

**1 pint (2 cups) medium
select oysters
¼ cup melted butter or
butter substitute
½ t. light salt
¼ t. black pepper
1 can Campbell's cream of
celery soup**

**1 t. finely chopped parsley
1 cup toasted white bread
crumbs
½ cup white cracker
crumbs**

1. Preheat oven to 425 degrees.
2. Drain oysters and set aside, reserving liquor in separate bowl.
3. Mix crumbs and butter, adding, salt, pepper and parsley. Set aside.
4. Heat to the boiling point the Cream of Celery Soup and oyster liquor.
5. Using a small whisk, beat out any lumps until mixture is smooth.
6. Spray a 9 inch oval pyrex dish or a 8 x 12 oblong with a No-Stick Spray, or grease well with margarine.
7. Layer one third of crumb mixture in bottom of dish.
8. Cover with one half of oysters and one half of soup/oyster liquor mixture.
9. Layer lightly a second third of crumb mixture, reserving enough crumbs for final topping.
10. Use all remaining oysters for next layer and rest of soup mixture.
11. Top with remaining crumb mixture, spreading evenly.
12. Bake at 425 degrees for 10-15 minutes, or until slightly brown.
13. Keep hot in warm oven or on electric hot plate until serving time, but do not prolong cooking.

English Peas In Consommé

Serves 4…double if serving 8

1 10 oz. package frozen green peas
½ cup water
1 scoop instant chicken bouillon or 1 chicken bouillon cube

¼ t. Italian Herb Seasoning
¼ t. black pepper coarsely ground
1 T. butter (or butter substitute)

1. Bring ½ cup water to a boil.
2. Add 1 scoop instant chicken bouillon or 1 chicken bouillon cube, Italian Herb Seasoning, pepper, and butter.
3. Stir until bouillon is dissolved.
4. Add frozen peas, cover, and bring to a boil.
5. Reduce heat to medium and cook 2 minutes only.
6. Remove from heat and let stand 5 minutes.
7. Serve peas in a heated bowl.

Deliciously Different Cranberry Conserve

Freezes beautifully...Will hold for over a month!
Makes 7 cups
Serves 12-14

**6 cups or 2 12-ounce
packages whole fresh
cranberries**
**4½ cups dark brown sugar
firmly packed**
**2½ cups white onion rings
sliced thin**

¾ cup water
1½ T. salt
**¼ t. coarsely ground black
pepper**
3 T. Worcestershire sauce

1. In a large saucepan, combine cranberries, brown sugar, onion rings, and ¾ cup of water.
2. Place over medium heat and stir until sugar is dissolved.
3. Reduce heat to a low simmer. Add salt and black pepper. Cook 10 minutes, stirring occasionally, or until cramberries are just tender.
4. Remove from heat and stir in 3 T. Worcestershire sauce.
5. Cool and pour into jars. Refrigerate or freeze until ready to use.

Piquant Pineapple Almond Salad

(See Rule for Congealed Salads, p. 229.)
Make ahead–will keep well for a week
Serves 10-12

2 envelopes plain gelatin
½ cup cold water
1 cup boiling water
½ cup cold water
½ cup cidar vinegar
½ t. salt
2 cups sugar
2 -3 drops green food
coloring

1 cup toasted almond
slivers*
1 cup diced sweet pickles
1 15½ oz. can crushed
pineapple, WELL
DRAINED
1 cup sliced stuffed olives

1. In a small mixing bowl sprinkle gelatin over ½ cup cold water and let sit for 2 minutes.

2. Add 1 cup boiling water and stir until dissolved.

3. Add ½ cup cold water, ½ cup vinegar, ½ t. salt, 2 cups sugar, and 2 to 3 drops green food coloring. Stir until well mixed and refrigerate until cold, but not set up– approximately 30 to 45 minutes.

4. Fold in almonds, sweet pickles, well drained pineapple, and olives.

5. Pour into lightly oiled individual molds, a 9 x 13 Pyrex dish, or a 1½ to 2 qt. salad mold or ring.

6. Cover mold with plastic wrap or aluminum foil and refrigerate until ready to serve.

7. Serve on a bed of lettuce, top with Sour Cream Dressing, p. 86, or mayonnaise. Sprinkle lightly with paprika for color and garnish with a parsley sprig.

Sour Cream Dressing

Serves 10-12

⅔ cup sour cream or "Lite" sour cream   **⅓ cup mayonnaise or "Lite" mayonnaise**

1. Mix together sour cream and mayonnaise.
2. Refrigerate until ready to use.

Toasted Almonds

These can be done weeks in advance and frozen.
Nice to have on hand.

1 2 ounce package slivered almonds   **1 t. butter**
¼ -½ t. salt (optional)

1. Preheat oven to 300 degrees.
2. Spread almonds out in a shallow pan.
3. Dot with butter and lightly salt.
4. Heat 8-10 minutes until lightly browned, stirring once.

HOT ROLLS

In by gone days, it would have been considered sinful to sit down to Christmas dinner without offering hot rolls. However, today's diet conscious diners may prefer seconds of dressing and gravy as a substitute for rolls. The following recipe comes from a famous old cook known for her delectable rolls. The other option is to choose from the many delicious varieties available in the grocery.

Bea's Famous Rolls

Freeze well
Makes 50 Parker House rolls

½ cup Crisco
¼ cup sugar
1 t. salt
1½ cups milk
1 package dry yeast (buy a
strip of 3 and use only 1)

1 egg, slightly beaten
3 cups All Purpose
pre-sifted flour
Melted butter

1. In a large mixing bowl, combine Crisco, sugar, and salt.
2. Heat 1½ cups milk until very hot. Do Not Boil.
3. Pour milk over sugar/Crisco mixture and stir until blended. Set aside until mixture is lukewarm. This step is important.
4. Fold in egg and yeast. Let set 2-3 minutes.
5. Begin adding flour, a little at a time, and knead dough until it doesn't stick to your hands. Add additional flour if needed.
6. Lightly grease top of dough with Crisco. Put bowl in a warm (not hot) place away from any draft. Let dough rise until it doubles in bulk.

Continued on next page

7. Take hands and punch down. Roll out dough ½ inch thick on a floured board or counter. Cut out rolls with a 2 inch diameter cookie cutter or use an empty 6 ounce can of tomato paste for cutting.
8. Paint each roll with melted butter, top and bottom, and fold over. Punch down to secure.
9. Place one inch apart on a well greased cookie sheet and let raise again—about 1½ hours.
10. Preheat oven to 425 degrees. Bake 15-20 minutes or until golden brown.

Ambrosia

A Refreshing Holiday Favorite of the Old South
Serves 8

6 large naval oranges
2 cups freshly grated cocoanut or 2 packages flake-grated, naturally moist frozen cocoanut (1 6 ounce frozen makes 1 cup grated-no canned)

½ cup sugar, or to taste
¼ cup orange juice
1 6 ounce jar of red maraschino cherries, drained

1. Carefully peel and section oranges with a sharp knife, removing white membrane.
2. Cut into small pieces and place a third in a serving dish.
3. Sprinkle with a third of the sugar and cocoanut. Repeat layers twice.
4. Pour orange juice over the ambrosia and let stand in refrigerator several hours before serving. Top with cherries before serving.

Note: Canned or fresh pineapple bits can be added.
Note: For a different flavor a little dry sherry can be mixed with the orange juice.

Menu II

"The Classic Victorian"

Tray of Celery and Stuffed Olives

Succulent Roast Duckling

with Fruit Stuffing

Orange Sauce

French Green Beans with Slivered Almonds

Steamed Wild Rice

Cranberry Salad

with Sour Cream Dressing

Hot Poppy Seed Rolls (optional)

Red and White Wines

English Plum Pudding

with Peach Brandy Sauce

Coffee

Duck A L'Orange

Serves 4 generously—buy 2 ducks if serving 8

1 4-5 lb. duckling	1 14½ oz. can Swanson's
1 t. salt	Chicken broth
2 T. butter	1 cup dry white wine
2 T. flour	

Fruit Stuffing

¼ cup butter or butter substitute	½ cup white seedless raisins
¾ cup orange juice	2 large tart apples, peeled and diced (Granny Smith's preferred)
2 T. orange marmalade	
1 8 oz. package Pepperidge Farm herb-seasoned dressing	

Orange Sauce

½ cup sugar	1 cup orange juice
½ cup water	1 cup fresh lemon juice
12 slivers orange rind	¼ cup brandy

DUCK A L'ORANGE

1. Preheat oven to 450 degrees.
2. Remove giblets and liver from duck and discard.
3. Wash duck inside and out. Pat dry and set aside.

PREPARE FRUIT STUFFING

1. Heat butter and orange juice in sauce pan until butter is melted.
2. Stir in marmalade, dressing, raisins, and diced apples.
3. Remove from heat and toss lightly until well mixed.
4. Stuff duck lightly with Fruit Stuffing. DO NOT OVERSTUFF–dressing will expand. Set aside extra dressing. Close opening with a skewer or sew up.
5. Rub duck with 1 t. salt and prick duck with a sharp fork all over to allow fat to drain.
6. Place duck breast side up on a rack in an uncovered roasting pan.
7. Bake for 20 minutes at 450 degrees.

PREPARE ORANGE SAUCE
(While duck is browning)

1. Bring ½ cup sugar and ½ cup water to boil.
2. Reduce to medium heat and let simmer until liquid is reduced and sugar/water combination turns light brown in color.
3. Add 12 slivers orange rind, 1 cup orange juice, 1 cup fresh lemon juice, and ¼ cup brandy. (NOTE: THE SUGAR/WATER MIXTURE WILL HARDEN WHEN THE JUICES ARE ADDED, BUT WILL MELT DOWN WHEN COOKED)
4. Stir and turn on low heat. Cook for 30 minutes stirring occasionally. Remove orange slivers and set pan aside.

REMOVE DUCKLING FROM ROASTING PAN AT END OF 20 MINUTES–SET ON PAPER TOWELS OR PLATTER TO CATCH THE DRIPPINGS

Continued on next page

1. Turn oven to 350 degrees.
2. Drain off all but 1 T. fat from roasting pan. Place pan over low heat on cook top.
3. Add 1 T. butter (or butter substitute) and 2 T. flour. Stir until blended.
4. Stir in chicken broth and white wine, cooking until slightly thickened.
5. Return duck to pan WITHOUT roasting rack. Cook 1 to 1½ hours, basting occasionally.
6. Lightly grease a casserole dish and place remaining stuffing in dish. Bake covered for last 30 minutes duck is cooking.
7. Duck will be done when meat thermometer reaches 185 degrees or when legs move easily.

PRESENTATION

1. Remove duck to serving platter and let sit 15 minutes before carving.
2. Add sauce from roasting pan to orange sauce mixture. Stir and heat to a medium boil. Add salt and pepper to taste. Set aside until ready to serve.
3. Garnish duck with seedless red and green grapes, orange wedges, and parsley.
4. Pass hot orange sauce in a sauce boat when ready to serve.

French Green Beans with Slivered Almonds

Double or triple for 8-12

1 10 oz. package frozen French-style green beans
1 T. butter

1 2 oz. package slivered almonds, toasted
salt
1 t. butter

1. Cook green beans according to directions. Drain well and set aside.
2. At serving time quickly re-warm green beans and toss with 1 T. melted butter.
3. Sprinkle with slivered almonds.

Note: Can substitute packaged frozen French-style green beans containing Almonds in Butter Sauce.

Toasted Slivered Almonds

Note: These can be done weeks in advance and frozen. Good to have on hand.

1. Spread almonds out on shallow pan.
2. Dot with 1 t. butter and lightly sprinkle with salt.
3. Heat in 300 degree oven until lightly browned, 8-10 minutes.

Steamed Wild Rice

Make ahead of time
Serves 6

1 box Uncle Ben's Long Grain and Wild Rice Mixture

2⅓ cups water
1 T. butter

1. Put water and butter into saucepan and bring to boil.
2. Stir contents of box and bring to boil.
3. Cover tightly and reduce to simmer.
4. Cook 23 minutes. (This can be done ahead to this point)
5. Reheat 5 minutes prior to serving.

Cranberry Salad

A colorful gem of a salad
Make ahead–keeps well for a week
See rule for congealed salads, p. 229.
Serves 8

1 3¾ ounce package lemon jello
1½ cups boiling water
1 cup sugar
1 12 ounce package whole fresh cranberries ground

1 cup chopped celery (approximately 2 stalks)
½ heaping cup chopped pecans

1. Rinse cranberries under cold water and let drain.
2. Spray 8 individual molds or one 8 x 12 pyrex dish with pam or a "non stick" spray.
3. In a medium size mixing bowl, dissolve Jello in 1½ cups boiling water. Add sugar and stir until all ingredients are well dissolved.
4. Coarsely chop cranberries in a food processor or blender. If using a blender, do not add water. Put one cup cranberries at a time in a blender. Blend on highest power, and remove. Repeat process until all cranberries are ground.
5. Add cranberries, chopped celery, and chopped pecans to Jello mixture. Stir to mix well.
6. Spoon into individual molds or one 8 x 12 pyrex dish.
7. Cover and refrigerate until ready to serve.
8. Serve on a bed of fresh lettuce and top with sour cream dressing. Sprinkle with paprika and garnish with a bud of parsley.

Sour Cream Dressing

Make ahead–keeps well for 3 weeks
Serves 10-12

¾ cup sour cream   **⅓ cup mayonnaise (no substitutes)**

1. Mix together sour cream and mayonnaise until well blended.
2. Refrigerate until ready to use.

Hot Poppy Seed Rolls

Make the day before

1 package Pepperidge Farm Party rolls or bakery equivalent   **Poppy Seeds Butter**

1. Preheat oven to 350 degrees.
2. Split rolls in half.
3. Butter each half and sprinkle lightly with poppy seeds. Cover tightly until ready to heat.
4. Heat 3-5 minutes until warm and butter has melted or run under broiler until crisp and browned.

English Plum Pudding

Make up to 6 weeks ahead
Serves 24

For generations in our family, this Christmas specialty
has been "the grand finale" to yet another memorable
Christmas dinner. Served on a gleaming silver tray, garnished
with fresh holly, and flamed at the table, family and friends
eagerly await the prize hidden somewhere in the pudding.
Before steaming, insert a nut or a tiny figure in the batter;
tradition has it that the person who finds it will have good
health and good luck throughout the coming year!

PART I

1 pound seedless raisins
1 pound currants
½ pound citron

¼ cup English walnuts
broken into pieces
1 cup All Purpose Pre-
Sifted Flour

PART II

1½ cups All Purpose
Pre-Sifted Flour
2 t. baking soda
½ t. ground cloves (add ½
t. more if you want
stronger flavor of cloves)

1 t. ground allspice
1 t. ground nutmeg
1 t. ground cinnamon
2 t. salt

PART III

4 eggs beaten
1 cup sugar
2 cups molasses
2 cups buttermilk
½ cup Crisco
½ cup Cointreau
2½ cups bread crumbs

1 small nut, unshelled, or 1
small figure to be
inserted into batter
before steaming.
(optional)
Candied cherries and holly
for garnish

PART I

1. Combine raisins, currants, citron, and walnuts in a medium size bowl.
2. Sprinkle with 1 cup flour and stir together. Set aside.

PART II

1. Combine all ingredients in Part II in another bowl. Stir until well blended. Set aside.

PART III

1. In a large mixing bowl, combine all ingredients in Part III. Stir until thoroughly mixed.
2. Add Parts I and II to ingredients in mixing bowl containing Part III.
3. Stir to mix thoroughly.
4. Grease the inside of two three pound molds (coffee cans, bundt pans, or large round pyrex baking dish) and sprinkle with sugar.
5. Pour pudding mixture in—ONLY ⅔rds full.
6. Place a tight fitting lid on molds or cans—aluminum foil secured with tight fitting string or rubber band will do.
7. Place on a rack in a roaster, heavy kettle, or Dutch oven. Pour boiling water halfway up on mold in bottom of roaster and cover tightly with lid.
8. Bring water to a boil. Reduce to simmer and steam about 3 to 3½ hours or until tester comes out clean. Add more boiling water if needed. Remove from roaster, cool 5 minutes, or bake 350 degrees for 3-3½ hours in oven. IN BOTH COOKING METHODS WATER SHOULD BE BARELY SIMMERING WHILE STEAMING.
9. Dribble ⅛ cup Cointreau over top and sides of each pudding.
10. Wrap tightly in foil and store in a cool, dry place until ready to serve.
11. Serve, flaming, with Peach Brandy Sauce, p. 98, or adorn with tiny red candles lit.

Peach Brandy Sauce

Make ahead and refrigerate–keeps well one week
Makes 4 cups

1 cup sugar
2 sticks (1 cup) softened
butter or butter
substitute
4 well beaten egg yolks

1 cup hot coffee cream
1 cup Peach Flavored
Brandy
Pinch of salt

In a 2 quart saucepan:

1. Mix together sugar and butter. Let butter melt and stir until sugar and butter are well blended.
2. Add 4 well beaten egg yolks and 1 cup warm cream. Stir until blended.
3. Cook slowly on medium low, stirring constantly, until it thickens. Do Not Boil.
4. Add 1 cup Peach Flavored Brandy and a pinch of salt if needed. Stir.
5. Remove from stove and cool. Sauce will be runny after addition of brandy.
6. Reheat before serving.

TO FLAME PUDDING

Flaming Plum Pudding is a dazzling finale to a beautiful Christmas dinner. Do not be intimidated–it's really quite simple if you follow the rules.

1. Heat ¼ cup Cointreau or Brandy until very hot, BUT NOT BOILING.
2. Pour warmed liqueur evenly over top of pudding and ignite immediately.
3. When flame has died out, slice pudding, and spoon Peach Brandy Sauce over each serving. Place a small sprig of holly on each plate for a festive ending.

Menu III

Tray of Celery and Stuffed Olives

Glazed, Spiral-Sliced, Ready to Serve Ham

with

Mustard Sauce

Roast Turkey Supreme

Giblet Gravy

Herbed Cornbread Dressing Balls

Jellied Cranberry Sauce

Artichoke and Spinach Casserole

Christmas Ribbon Salad

Hot Buttered Rolls

Fruit Cake Slices

GLAZED, SPIRAL SLICED, READY TO SERVE HAM

Many a candle has burned brightly beside the traditional holiday ham, ever a symbol of Yuletide hospitality. Today's hostess has a wide choice of hams, boned, trimmed and cooked to full tenderness and flavor, spiral sliced and ready to serve.

TO HEAT HAM

It is not necessary to heat the ham. Let come to room temperature and serve with warm MUSTARD SAUCE. If you do wish, however, to serve warm, follow the directions below.

1. Preheat oven to 325 degrees.
2. Place ham on a rack, uncovered, in a shallow pan.
For a whole ham allow 15 to 18 minutes per pound. For a half ham, allow 18 to 24 minutes per pound.

Mustard Sauce

A delicious sweet-sour sauce.
Make ahead–keeps 3 weeks in refrigerator

1 beef bouillon cube
1 cup boiling water
2 T. butter or butter
   substitute
1 cup cider vinegar

½ cup sugar
2 T. flour
2 eggs beaten slightly
½ T. dry mustard

In a small saucepan:
1. Dissolve bouillon cube in 1 cup boiling water.
2. Add 2 T. butter and let melt. Add vinegar.
3. Combine sugar, flour, eggs, and mustard in small mixing bowl. Mix well. Pour a small amount of hot bouillon liquid into flour/egg mixture. Stir. Mix well and add to saucepan.
4. Cook over low heat, stirring, until thickened. (About 6-8 minutes)
5. Serve warm.* Refrigerate leftover sauce to use with sandwiches.

*To reheat, place sauce in a glass serving dish in a small amount of simmering water. Stir until heated throughout.

Roast Turkey Supreme

See p. 75 for recipe.

Read "ALL ABOUT TURKEY" p.70-72.

Giblet Gravy

See p. 79 for recipe.

Herbed Cornbread Dressing Balls

Make ahead and freeze—let come to room temperature before cooking

Makes 16-17 individual 2½-3 inch balls

1 8 ounce package Pepperidge Farm Corn Bread Stuffing
1 stick butter or butter substitute
½ cup hot water or chicken broth
1 cup finely chopped celery
1 cup finely chopped white onion

1½ t. Sage
⅛ t. salt
¾ t. pepper
1 beaten egg (optional) if extra moist dressing preferred
2 -3 T. melted butter for brushing dressing balls before cooking

1. Preheat oven to 350 degrees.
2. Melt butter.
3. Add corn bread stuffing, hot water or chicken broth, chopped celery, chopped onion, sage, salt, and pepper. Add beaten egg if wish. Mix well until all ingredients are well blended.
4. Form into balls about the size of an ice cream scoop.
5. Brush with melted butter.
6. Place on a cookie sheet and bake 30 minutes at 350 degrees.
7. Dressing balls will be crunchy on the outside. May be held in a warm oven for an hour—cover with aluminum foil if holding.

Jellied Cranberry Sauce

Make ahead and freeze–but so easy can be made
at last minute
Makes 2½ cups

1 cup sugar
1 cup water

1 12 ounce package whole
fresh cranberries

1. Rinse cranberries with cold water and let drain.
2. In a sauce pan, mix sugar and water. Stir to dissolve sugar.
3. Bring sugar/water mixture to a boil. Add cranberries.
4. Reduce heat to medium low and simmer gently for 10 minutes. Stir occasionally.
5. Remove from heat and let cool.
6. Pour into serving dish and refrigerate until ready to serve.

Artichoke and Spinach Casserole

Can be made two days before serving and kept refrigerated—
let come to room temperature before cooking
Serves 8-10

2 10 ounce packages frozen chopped spinach, thawed and well drained
2 8 ounce cans artichoke hearts, drained and cut in half
¼ cup butter (½ stick) or butter substitute
2 T. milk
½ heaping cup finely chopped white onions
1 8 ounce package cream cheese, room temperature
1 8 ounce can sliced water chestnuts, drained
¼ t. salt
½ t. Knorr Swiss Aromat All-Purpose Seasoning
¼ t. Tabasco sauce
½ t. coarsely ground black pepper
14 individual saltine squares or ½ cup Pepperidge Farm Herb Seasoned Stuffing
1 T. butter for topping
Paprika

1. Preheat oven to 375 degrees.
2. In a sauce pan, melt ½ cup butter. Add milk, finely chopped onions, and cream cheese. Remove from heat and beat with whisk until creamy and smooth.
3. Add salt, Knorr Seasoning, tabasco, and black pepper. Stir to mix well.
4. Fold in well drained spinach and water chestnuts.
5. Lightly butter or spray with a "no stick" cooking spray a 9 x 13 baking dish.
6. Line bottom of baking dish with drained artichoke halves, then spread spinach mixture evenly over top of artichokes.

7. Crumble saltines over top or sprinkle with ½ cup Herb Seasoned Stuffing. Dot 1 T. butter over top and sprinkle lightly with paprika.
8. Bake 375 degrees for 30-35 minutes or until casserole is heated throughout. Can run under broiler to brown top if desired.

MICROWAVE DIRECTIONS

Cover casserole with plastic wrap leaving vent space on both ends of dish. Microwave medium high power (7) 12-14 minutes or until casserole is heated throughout. Turn dish at ½ cooking time. Let stand 5 minutes before serving.

Christmas Ribbon Ring Salad

Delicious and festive with layers of red and green separated
by a band of white
Make ahead–keeps well for a week–or freeze and let thaw in
refrigerator overnight before unmolding
see rule for congealed salads, p. 229.
Serves 14

LAYER I

1 3 ounce package
  raspberry jello
¾ cup boiling water

1 1 pound can whole
  cranberry sauce

LAYER II

1 3 ounce package
  lemon jello
1 cup boiling water
1 8 ounce package cream
  cheese, room
  temperature

1 15½ ounce can crushed
  pineapple, undrained
½ cup chopped pecans

LAYER III

1 3 ounce package
  lime jello
¾ cup boiling water
1 11 ounce can mandarin
  orange segments,
  undrained (can should
  contain ½ cup orange
  juice)

1 8 ounce box chopped
  dates

LAYER I

1. Spray 14 individual molds, 1 2 quart salad mold, or 1 13 x 9 inch baking dish with a "no stick cooking spray" or coat molds lightly with vegetable oil.
2. Dissolve raspberry jello in ¾ cup boiling water. Stir until thoroughly dissolved.
3. Add cranberry sauce and mix thoroughly with dissolved jello.
4. Pour into mold or divide evenly among 14 individual molds.
5. Refrigerate until almost set.

LAYER II

1. Dissolve lemon jello in 1 cup boiling water. Stir until thoroughly dissolved.
2. Pour mixture into blender. Add cream cheese and undrained pineapple. Blend until smooth. If blender is not available, beat by hand or with electric mixer until smooth.
3. Stir in ½ cup chopped pecans.
4. Pour over cranberry layer in mold. Chill until almost firm.

LAYER III

1. Dissolve lime jello in ¾ cup of boiling water. Stir until thoroughly dissolved.
2. Add mandarin orange segments, undrained, and chopped dates.
3. Pour over cheese layer.
4. Cover with plastic wrap or aluminum foil and chill until set.
5. Unmold on a bed of lettuce, garnish with parsley, and serve with Sour Cream Dressing.

Sour Cream Dressing

Make ahead–keeps well for 2-3 weeks
Makes 1 cup–serves 10-12

**⅔ cup sour cream or
"Lite Sour Cream"**

**⅓ cup mayonnaise or "Lite
Mayonnaise–no other
substitutes**

1. Mix together sour cream and mayonnaise until well blended.
2. Refrigerate until ready to use.

Hot Buttered Rolls

See p. 87 for Bea's Famous Rolls or p. 95 for Hot Poppy Seed Rolls

Fruit Cake Slices

Slice fruit cake, p. 175, place on glass or silver tray, decorate with sprigs of holly and red and green cherries

SAVORING THAT LEFT OVER TURKEY
DON'T THROW AWAY THOSE
TURKEY BONES!

Christmas turkey stages an encore in seven
captivating recipes

SAVORING THAT LEFT OVER TURKEY DON'T THROW AWAY THOSE TURKEY BONES!

Turkey Broth
Don't Wash the Roaster!

Nutritious and tasty—save for soup and stock in
the following recipes

1 meaty, cooked turkey carcass	**1 cup parsley (if available)**
2-3 quarts cold water	**all left over dressing**
1-2 onions, peeled and cut in half	**all left over gravy**
3 stalks celery with leaves	**1 bay leaf**
	2 t. salt
	1 t. pepper

1. Debone turkey saving all good meat for left-overs. Wrap meat in plastic wrap or aluminum foil. Refrigerate or freeze. If frozen, package in meal-size portions. Put in ziplock freezer bags and place in freezer.
2. In same roasting pan, place all meaty turkey bones broken up, all skin, onions, celery, parsley, any left over dressing and gravy, bay leaf, salt, and pepper.
3. Cover with 2-3 quarts of cold water.
4. Bring to a boil, reduce heat to simmer, stir, and cover with lid (or use aluminum foil if using a foil roaster).
5. Let broth simmer 8-10 hours—can cook all night on lowest heat.
6. Strain broth, reserving only the strained liquid. Discard everything else.
7. Refrigerate and let fat come to top.
8. Remove fat either by lifting with spatula or knife. Discard fat.
9. Divide fat skimmed broth among jars, leaving 1 inch headroom for expansion; label and freeze.

Pasta Soup

Serves 4 heartily

**4 cups seasoned and
thickened turkey broth
(see note below if broth
is too thin)
1 10 ounce can stewed
tomatoes, undrained
(Contadina or Pregresso
preferred)**

**½ cup chopped onion
¾ cup chopped celery
2 cups (more if desired)
Rigatini or any small
pasta)
Salt and pepper to taste**

1. In a large soup kettle or sauce pan, bring 4 cups turkey broth to a boil.
2. Add tomatoes, chopped onion and celery. Stir and reduce heat to a medium simmer. Cook 10 to 15 minutes or until onion and celery are almost done.
3. Add pasta and cook 4 to 5 minutes or length of time according to package directions. Season to taste with salt and pepper if desired.
4. Serve in warm soup bowls.

TO THICKEN BROTH: Mix 1 T. cornstarch with ¼ cup cold water and add to soup, or mix in ¼ cup instant mashed potatoes with soup broth.

Turkey Imperial

A quick and easy gourmet treat–freezes well
(Cook wild rice ahead of time and reheat)
Serves 4-6

4 cups cubed and cooked turkey meat (preferably a mixture of white and dark for better flavor)
4 T. butter or butter substitute
4 T. all purpose flour
2 cups hot turkey broth or 2 cups canned chicken broth (Swanson's preferred)
½ cup finely minced onion
½ pound (15 whole) fresh mushrooms, halved. Add stems.
¼ t. freshly ground black pepper
¼ t. salt
⅛ t. Tabasco
¼ cup dry sherry
½ cup toasted almonds, slivered
Long Grain and Wild Rice

1. Melt butter and add flour. Stir until smooth.
2. Pour hot turkey or chicken broth into butter/flour mixture and stir until smooth.
3. Add onions, mushroom, salt, pepper, and Tabasco. Cook over medium low heat, stirring, for 10 minutes.
4. Add turkey and sherry. Stir to mix well.
5. Serve over bed of wild rice, garnish with almonds and a sprig of parsley.

Long Grain and Wild Rice

(make ahead of time)
See recipe, p. 93
Serves 4-6

Turkey Olé

Mexican Super Supper
Serves 4 heartily

2 cups cooked turkey, cut in bite size chunks

1 can cream of chicken soup

1 4 oz. can mild green chopped chilies, undrained

½ heaping cup chopped onion

½ cup black olives sliced in half

¼ t. coarsley ground black pepper

Scant ⅛ t. garlic powder

1 8 ounce carton sour cream or Lite sour cream

2 cups crushed Nacho Cheese Flavored Tortilla chips

1 cup shredded Monterey Jack Cheese

1. Preheat oven to 350 degrees.
2. Grease an 8 x 8 baking dish or casserole dish of similar size.
3. Combine turkey chunks, soup, undrained chilies, chopped onion, olives, pepper, and garlic powder. Stir to mix well.
4. Layer as follows: Sprinkle 1 cup of crushed Tortilla chips on bottom, spread half of soup/turkey mixture over chips, top with one half of sour cream, and 1 cup tortilla chips. Spread rest of soup mixture over chips, top with rest of sour cream, and sprinkle 1 cup shredded Monterey Jack Cheese on top.
5. Bake 350 for 30 minutes or until cheese is melted and casserole is hot throughout.
6. Let sit 5-10 minutes before serving.

Cashew Turkey Casserole

(Can substitute chicken–see p. 120 for chicken)
Serves 6

2 cups cooked turkey (or chicken) cut into bite size chunks
1 can Cream of Mushroom soup
½ cup chicken broth*
1 16 ounce can Chop Suey Vegetables, drained
1 8 ounce can sliced water chestnuts, drained

¾ cup Cashew nuts
1 cup chopped green pepper
2 t. minced dried onion
¼ t. Tabasco
⅛ t. curry powder
3 cups Chow Mein Noodles

1. Preheat oven to 375 degrees.
2. Mix turkey, soup, chicken broth, Chop Suey Vegetables, water chestnuts, cashew nuts, green pepper, minced onion, Tabasco, and curry powder together. Stir to mix well.
3. Fold in 2 cups Chow Mein Noodles.
4. Spoon into a lightly greased (or spray with a "no stick cooking spray") 2 quart casserole dish.
5. Sprinkle remaining 1 cup Chow Mein Noodles over top.
6. Bake 375 degrees for 20 minutes or until hot throughout. Let sit 5 minutes before serving.

*If no chicken broth on hand, dissolve 1 chicken bouillon cube or 1 scoop instant chicken bouillon in ¾ cup hot water–use one half cup of this for casserole.

Lasagna Florentine con Tacchino

(Lasagna with Turkey and Spinach)
An easy and delicious pasta–
Chicken can be substituted for turkey.
See p. 120.
Serves 10

Prepare Ahead!

Dice 4 cups turkey, eliminating all skin. Refrigerate. Defrost, drain, and squeeze all liquid out of 2 10 oz. packages frozen chopped spinach.

INGREDIENTS FOR PASTA

6 cups boiling water
½ t. salt
1 t. olive or corn oil

8 oz. lasagna noodles
(½ box)

INGREDIENTS FOR SAUCE

½ cup butter (1 stick) or
butter substitute
¼ cup flour
2 cups Swansons
Chicken Broth
(1 14½ ounce can)
½ t. salt
¼ t. coarsely ground black
pepper

¾ t. dried basil
2 large cloves garlic,
pressed or finely minced
¼ t. Tabasco
4 cups diced cooked
turkey* (no skin)

INGREDIENTS FOR SPINACH FILLING

2 cups Ricotta cheese
(1 15 oz. container) or 2
cups small curd cottage
cheese, well drained
1 egg slightly beaten
2 10 oz. packages frozen
chopped spinach,
thawed and well drained

½ t. salt
¼ t. coarsely ground black
pepper

CHEESE

2 cups crumbled Mozzarella cheese

6 T. freshly grated Parmesan cheese

1. Preheat oven to 350 degrees.
2. Bring 6 cups water to a rapid boil, adding ½ t. salt, and 1 t. olive or corn oil.
3. Drop lasagna into boiling water. Boil, uncovered, 10 minutes only. DO NOT OVERCOOK. At end of 10 minutes, drain and rinse with cold water. (This eliminates starch.)
4. While lasagna is cooking, melt ½ cup butter (1 stick) in a 2 quart sauce pan over low heat.
5. When butter is melted, stir in ¼ cup flour and whisk to blend.
6. Add chicken broth, salt, pepper, basil, garlic, and Tabasco. Whisk to blend all ingredients.
7. Cook slowly, stirring, until sauce is slightly thickened; about 8-10 minutes. Remove from heat and add 4 cups diced turkey. Stir and set aside.
8. In a small bowl mix well: slightly beaten egg, ricotta, well drained spinach, salt and pepper. Set aside.
9. Lightly grease a 9 x 13 pyrex baking dish.
10. Layer as follows: Place one half of lasagna noodles on bottom, top with one half sauce mixture. Spread one half of Ricotta/spinach filling on top of sauce. Sprinkle with 1 cup of Mozzrella cheese and 3 T. Parmesan. Repeat layers ending up with cheese on top.
12. Bake 30-40 minutes at 350 degrees or until hot and bubbly throughout. Let stand 10-15 minutes before serving to set.

*Chicken can be substituted for turkey. Recipe will require approximately 1½ pounds cooked and skinless chicken breasts. "HOW TO COOK CHICKEN BREASTS FOR TETRAZZINI AND LASAGNA", p. 120.

Dixie Shortcake

(Chicken breasts can be substituted–see p. 120.)
Serves 4

4 squares cornbread (see recipe p. 19)
2 cups cooked sliced or diced turkey, room temperature
6 slices bacon fried and crumbled

2 T. butter or butter substitute
2 T. All purpose flour
1 14 oz. can Swanson's chicken broth
1 t. dry Sherry
Salt and pepper to taste

1. Make cornbread, p. 19, cut in large squares. Split four squares and set aside. Freeze remaining cornbread.
2. Make gravy. (If well seasoned turkey gravy is already made, use 2 cups instead of preparing gravy.)
3. Melt butter in small sauce pan. Add flour, whisking well to blend.
4. Add chicken broth, stirring until all ingredients are well blended and gravy has thickened to desired consistency. Cook on medium to medium low.
5. Add sherry and taste. Add salt and pepper if needed.
6. Top cornbread squares with turkey, pour ¼ cup gravy over each square, and sprinkle bacon evenly over all.

Quick Turkey Tetrazinni

Make ahead supper buffet–freezes well
Substitute chicken if turkey not available
See p. 120 if substituting chicken
Serves 8

6 cups water
½ t. salt
1 T. olive or cooking oil
1 8 oz. package spaghetti
  broken into pieces
2-2½ cups cooked diced
  chicken or turkey
1 4 oz. can mushrooms,
  undrained
1 T. minced dried onions
¼ t. Tabasco
¼ t. marjoram

1 10¾ oz. can Cream of
  Chicken soup
1 13 oz. can evaporated
  milk
1 4 oz. package grated
  sharp Cheddar cheese
½ cup grated Parmesan
  cheese
2 T. chopped pimento
  (optional)
2 T. dry sherry (optional)

1. Put 6 cups water on to boil, adding salt and oil.
2. Drop spaghetti into boiling water and cook 18 minutes.
3. Drain mushrooms and reserve liquid.
4. While spaghetti is cooking, put into large mixing bowl: mushroom liquid, minced onion, Tabasco, marjoram, Cream of Chicken soup, and evaporated milk.
5. Mix until ingredients are well blended.
6. Add mushrooms, chicken, and pimento, mixing well.
7. Drain spaghetti and rinse under cold water. (This eliminates starch.)
8. Divide spaghetti into 3 equal parts.
9. Cover bottom of a 9 x 13 inch pyrex dish with layers of: a third of spaghetti, half the chicken mixture, and half the sharp cheese; repeat, ending up with layer of spaghetti.
10. Sprinkle ½ cup Parmesan cheese over top.
11. Bake 30 minutes at 400 degrees or until hot and bubbly. Let set 10 minutes before serving.

To Cook Chicken For Lasagna, Tetrazzini, or Any Recipe Calling for Turkey

CONVENTIONAL METHOD

6 chicken breasts, skinless
2 celery stalks
½ onion quartered

½ t. salt
¼ t. coarsely ground
black pepper

1. Cover chicken breasts, celery, onion with water.
2. Add salt and bring to a boil.
3. Cover tightly and let simmer on medium low heat until tender and meat falls off bone when pricked with a fork (approximately 20 minutes).
4. Let chicken cool in its own liquid.
5. Save liquid for soup or to cook pasta in recipes for tetrazzini or lasagna.

MICROWAVE METHOD

6 skinless chicken breasts
1 T. butter

salt and pepper

1. Lightly sprinkle salt and pepper over each chicken breast.
2. Melt 1 T. butter in pyrex dish large enough to hold chicken breasts.
3. Arrange chicken so that meatiest portions are to outside of dish.
4. Cover with wax paper and microwave on high 2 to 3 minutes per piece of chicken. Turn chicken over and repeat time for amount of pieces to be cooked.
5. TEST FOR DONENESS—CHICKEN SHOULD BE FORK TENDER WITH NO PINKNESS NEXT TO THE BONE. (For frozen chicken breasts, increase cooking time to 4 to 5 minutes per piece, turn over, and repeat.)

THE SPECIAL MAGIC OF NEW YEAR'S EVE

FAREWELL TO THE OLD!
HELLO TO THE NEW!
THE AFTER-MIDNIGHT BREAKFAST!

THE SPECIAL MAGIC OF NEW YEAR'S EVE

FAREWELL TO THE OLD!
HELLO TO THE NEW!

The party begins at 8 or 9—set up the bar early in the day; prepare ahead several of the easy appetizers (not too much, but just enough) to satisfy the hunger pangs until the clock chimes 12 and the "Midnight Breakfast" begins...

THE SPECIAL MAGIC OF NEW YEAR'S EVE

THE AFTER-MIDNIGHT BREAKFAST!

Eggs Fantastic
Cranapple Compote
Toasted English Muffins
or
Miniature Cinnamon Rolls

Surprise Quiche
Tangy Apricot Mold
Ginger Bread Raisin Muffins

Fancy Egg Scramble
with
Broccoli and Ham
Spiced Peach Halves
Blueberry Muffins

The Bar

Whatever the set-up, conviviality begins at the bar whether it be an impressive built-in or a card table covered with a brightly colored cloth or sheet.

Though popular drinks vary with region and season, basics are: Bourbon, Scotch, Vodka, Gin, and Rum. Add bottles of red and chilled white wines. And then the mixes: club soda, tonic, Tom Collins, ginger ale, Seven Up, and, also, some lemon peel and green unstuffed olives.

For non-drinkers and calorie counters there are the tonic water and sodas served with a twist of lemon peel over ice, plus delectable juices galore.

Fill a large ice chest with ice and slide under the table or be-side an improvised bar along with extra bottles. Allow 1 pound of ice per person. Bar "musts" are: ice bucket full of ice, large pitcher of ice water, highball glasses, wine glasses, jigger glasses, and spoons for stirring.

Count on average guest having 2-3 drinks using a 1½-ounce portion of liquor per drink.

Bottle Size and Servings

(Wine and Spirits are no longer sold in fifths, but metric bottles instead)

Spirits

BOTTLE SIZE	CORRESPONDS TO:	SERVES
1 750 milliliter (25.4 oz.)	a Fifth	16 1½ oz. portions
1 liter (33.8 oz.)	a Quart	22 1½ oz. portions
1.75liter (59.2 0z.)	a Half Gallon	39 1½ oz. portions

Wine

Estimated amounts are for a 4 ounce wine glass

1 750 milliliter bottle (25.4 oz.)	a Fifth	6
1 liter bottle (33.8 oz.)	a Quart	8
1 1.75 milliliter bottle (59.2 oz.)	a Half Gallon	14
1 CASE of CHAMPAGNE		72 servings

Jiffy Cheese Spread

Preparation time: 6 minutes
Makes 2 cups

**2 4 oz. package shredded
  sharp Cheddar cheese
3 T. mayonnaise (no
  substitutes)**

**6 green onions minced
  (more tops than bottoms)
1 t. Dijon mustard
½ t. Tabasco**

1. Mince onions finely.
2. Combine cheese, mayonnaise, onions, mustard, and Tabasco, mixing well.
3. Form into a mound.
4. Sprinkle with paprika, garnish with parsley, and serve with crackers.

Italian Tuna Spread

Preparation time: 6 minutes
Makes 2 cups

**1 7 oz. can white tuna
½ cup ripe olives
  (buy 3 oz. can)**

**1 package Good Seasons
  Italian Salad
  Dressing Mix
1 cup sour cream**

1. Drain off oil or water from tuna and rinse meat in cold water.
2. Cut olives in fourths.
3. Combine tuna, olives, salad dressing mix, and sour cream.
4. Stir until well mixed.
5. Place in serving dish, sprinkle with paprika, and serve with crackers.

Note: If no ripe olives on hand, omit.

Walkin' Tacos

With this hearty spread, you need little else except
some toasted nuts and perhaps a tray of cheese
or a jiffy cheese spread   Prepare a day or two before
Serves 20-25

1 9″ pie pan
1 can Frito Lay bean dip or
  other brand of equal
  quality
1 8 oz. carton sour cream or
  "lite sour cream"
1 package Taco Seasoning
  mix
½ cup mayonnaise (no
  substitutes except "lite
  mayonnaise")
1 4 ounce can chopped
  green chilies, drained
2 tomatoes, finely chopped
  and drained on a paper
  towel

6 green onions, chopped,
  tops also
1 can frozen avocado dip,
  thawed
1 ripe avocado, chopped
  coarsely (optional)
1 t. lemon juice
⅛ -¼ t. Tabasco sauce
  (depending upon taste)
1 4 oz. package sharp
  Cheddar cheese, grated
1 4 ounce can black olives,
  drained and chopped
Taco Flavored Dorito chips
  or dip size Fritos

1. Spread 1 can bean dip on bottom of a 9 inch pie pan.
2. Mix together: sour cream, Taco Seasoning mix,
   mayonnaise, and drained, chopped chilies. Whisk to blend
   well.
3. Spread sour cream mixture over top of bean dip.
4. Sprinkle chopped tomatoes and green onions over sour
   cream mixture.
5. Mix together: thawed avocado dip, chopped fresh
   avocado (optional), lemon juice, and Tabasco. Stir to mix
   well. Spread over tomato/onion layer.
6. Sprinkle grated Cheddar cheese over avocado layer and
   top with chopped black olives.
7. Cover tightly and refrigerate until ready to serve.
8. Garnish with parsley and serve with Taco Flavored Dorito
   chips or dip size Fritos, or toastados.

Frosted Braunschweiger Paté

An easy make ahead appetizer–freezes well
Serves 18-20

1 8" aluminum foil pie pan
1 8 ounce package cream cheese, or "lite" cream cheese softened
8 ounces braunschweiger
2 T. grated onion
1 T. Worcestershire sauce
1 T. lemon juice

2 ounces additional cream cheese, room temperature for frosting
2 T. mayonnaise (no substitutes)
1 4 oz. jar pimientos, drained, (optional)
Crackers and parsley

1. In a mixing bowl, combine cream cheese, braunschweiger, onion, Worcestershire sauce, and lemon juice. Blend until smooth.

2. Lightly butter an eight inch foil pie pan. Spoon mixture into pan, smooth out so that mixture is evenly distributed. Cover with plastic wrap or aluminum foil and place in freezer. Paté can be frozen at this point.
   If freezing, wrap tightly with freezer wrap on top of plastic wrap.

3. If serving immediately, let paté harden to almost freezing point. Invert on serving platter, twist sides of aluminum pie pan, and paté will slip out in a perfect mold. If frozen, follow same directions with frozen paté. Allow an hour at room temperature for defrosting.

4. While still hard on top, combine 2 ounces of cream cheese and 2 T. mayonnaise. Blend until smooth.

5. Frost top and sides of paté and decorate with pimiento strips and parsley for color.

6. Serve with crackers.

Continued on next page

NOTE: If available, place paté in a Christmas wreath or tree mold which have been lightly buttered. Unmold by placing a warm damp towel over bottom of frozen mold. If mold is aluminum foil, simply twist to disengage. Let paté slip out on serving platter. Frost and decorate with pimiento strips and parsley. Sprigs of holly are also pretty on this decorated mold.

Salmon Party Mold

Make ahead and freeze
Serves 18-20

1 16 oz. can pink salmon, deboned and drained
1 8 oz. package cream cheese or "lite" cream cheese, room temperature

⅛ t. garlic salt
¼ t. prepared horseradish
¼ t. lemon juice
French Onion Dip for topping

1. Lightly butter with margarine or spray with a "no stick" cooking spray 1 8″ aluminum (throw away) pie pan.
2. In a mixing bowl, combine salmon, cream cheese, garlic salt, horseradish, and lemon juice.
3. Mix well until salmon is broken up and all ingredients are well blended and texture is creamy. Can also use a food processor or mixer.
4. Spoon into pie pan, cover tightly and place in freezer.* When hard, gently bend sides of pie pan and let mold slip out on serving plate.
5. Spread French Onion Dip over top and sides, sprinkle with paprika for color, and garnish with sliced stuffed green olives and parsley. Serve with Ritz crackers.
* If freezing, do not add French Onion Dip until taken from freezer and ready to serve. Wrap well in plastic wrap or aluminum foil first, then tightly in freezer wrap.

Spicey Oyster Crackers

So simple—keeps well in freezer

¾ cup vegetable oil
1 small package ranch
dressing mix
1 t. garlic powder

1 t. dill weed
⅛ t. cayenne pepper
12 oz. package oysters
crackers

1. Mix all ingredients in an airtight container large enough to hold crackers when added. Stir to mix well.
2. Add crackers and shake well, coating crackers on all sides.
3. Let stand 3 hours, stirring or shaking often.
4. Place in freezer until ready to use. Not necessary to thaw before serving.

...FOR OTHER APPETIZERS...

Menu 1

Eggs Fantastic

Cranapple Compote

Toasted English Muffins

or

Miniature Cinnamon Rolls

Hot Coffee

Eggs Fantastic

Make the day before!
Serves 6-8

½ T. butter or butter substitute

1 pound Jimmy Dean's regular sausage, browned

⅛ t. Tabasco

½ pound fresh mushrooms, sliced (about 6-7 large mushrooms)

6 eggs

1 8 oz. carton sour cream or "lite" sour cream

3 T. chopped green onions, tops included

1 T. chopped fresh parsley or 1 t. dried parsley

½ t. ground cumin

½ t. salt

½ t. coarsley ground black pepper

1 8 oz. block Monterey Jack cheese, grated (approximately 2 heaping cups)

1 4 oz. can chopped green chilies, drained

8 T. Thick 'n Chunky "Mild" Salsa (substitute "Hot" if preferred)

1 cup (1 4 oz. package) grated sharp Cheddar cheese

STEP 1

1. Preheat oven to 400 degrees.
2. Place ½ T. butter in an 8 x 12 pyrex baking dish and put in oven.
3. When butter has melted, remove from oven and tilt dish so that butter paints sides and bottom of dish. Set aside.
4. In a large skillet, crumble and brown sausage over medium heat until sausage is completely cooked. Stir occasionally.
5. Add ⅛ t. Tabasco and sliced mushrooms. Reduce heat to low and cook 1-2 minutes, stirring. Remove from heat and drain off accumulated fat. Set aside.

STEP II

1. In a mixing bowl, combine eggs and sour cream. Whisk until blended.
2. To egg mixture add: chopped green onions, parsley, cumin, salt, and pepper.
3. Pour egg mixture into 8 x 12 baking dish and place in preheated 400 degree oven.
4. Bake until eggs are just softly set, 10-15 minutes. Stir several times from outside to center to keep eggs from setting up around outside of dish. Remove as soon as eggs are "just softly set". DO NOT OVERCOOK.

STEP III

If baking immediately, set oven temperature at 325 degrees

1. Sprinkle grated Monterey Jack cheese over egg layer.
2. Top with drained chilies.
3. Spoon sausage/mushroom mixture over cheese and chilies.
4. Spoon 8 T. salsa evenly over sausage layer and top with 1 cup grated sharp Cheddar cheese.
5. Cover and refrigerate until ready to bake. Let come to room temperature before baking.
6. Bake 325 degrees for 30 minutes or until cheeses are melted. Let sit 5-10 minutes before cutting.

Cranapple Compote

Festive in color—delicious in taste
Make ahead—keeps 3 weeks
Serves 10

1 12 ounce package
fresh cranberries
1 cup sugar
1 cup water
8 medium size tart
apples (Granny
Smith preferred)

1¼ cups sugar
2 cups water
¼ t. ground cinnamon

1. In a medium size saucepan, combine sugar and water. Bring to a boil. Add cranberries, reduce heat to medium. Cook until skins pop (about 10 minutes). Set aside.
2. Peel and slice 8 medium apples. Cut into wedges.
3. In a 2 quart saucepan, combine sugar, water, and cinnamon. Bring to a boil. Stir to mix well.
4. Reduce heat to a medium boil, add apples, and cook until just tender—pierce with a fork. Apples should be slightly resistant to fork and not mushy. Remove from heat and let cool.
5. Pour apples into a glass casserole dish. Add cranberry mixture to the top. DO NOT STIR UNTIL THE NEXT DAY!

Toasted English Muffins

Serves 8

8 English muffins **1 jar marmalade**
Butter

1. Split English muffins, tearing in half to give coarse texture.
2. Butter each half generously.
3. Place 6 inches from broiler flame.
4. Broil 6-8 minutes or until light golden brown.
5. Serve with marmalade.

Note: Wrap in foil and place in warm oven until ready to serve if prepared in advance.

If miniature cinnamon rolls are preferred, purchase from bakery, wrap in foil, and heat in a 300 degree oven for 10-15 minutes or until warm throughout. Serve with butter.

Menu II

Surprise Quiche

Tangy Apricot Mold

Ginger Bread Raisin Muffins

Hot Coffee

SURPRISE QUICHE

Differently delicious and so easy to prepare ahead
Serves 5 heartily-6 well
(if serving five, see directions on how to cut quiche
for 5 portions)

**1 9″ ready to bake
pie shell
4 eggs, beaten
1 cup ham diced in
small pieces
2 jars marinated artichoke
hearts, drained (Cara Mia
perferred)
1 clove garlic pressed or
finely minced
¼ salt**

**⅛ t. coarsely ground black
pepper
1 t. freeze dried chives
⅛ t. oregano
⅛ t. Tabasco
2 cups grated sharp
Cheddar cheese (buy 2 4
oz. packages sharp
cheddar, grated or grate a
one pound block and
freeze remainder for
future use)**

PREPARE EVERYTHING THE DAY BEFORE

1. Preheat oven to 400 degrees.
2. Let pie shell come to room temperature. With a fork, prick
bottom and sides all over.
3. Bake 8 to 10 minutes or until light golden brown. Check at
end of 8 minutes.
4. Remove from oven, let cool, cover, and set aside until ready
to fill.

DO NOT FILL UNTIL READY TO BAKE OR PIE SHELL
WILL BECOME SOGGY

Continued on next page

QUICHE FILLING

1. Put eggs in a medium size mixing bowl and beat with a whisk.
2. Add ham.
3. Quarter drained artichoke hearts and add to egg/ham mixture.
4. Add pressed or finely minced garlic, salt, pepper, chives, oregano, and Tabasco. Stir to mix well.
5. Fold in grated sharp cheese. Stir, and cover with plastic wrap. Refrigerate until ready to pour into pie shell.

WHEN READY TO BAKE

1. Preheat oven to 325 degrees.
2. Pour quiche filling into baked pie shell. Filling will look like almost too much for pie shell, but it cooks down.
3. Put in oven and bake 40-45 minutes or until filling is set in center. Let rest 10 minutes before slicing into serving pieces.

TO CUT A QUICHE FOR FIVE PEOPLE

1. Make a "Y" with a sharp pointed knife.

2. Then draw two other lines, making even slices.

Tangy Apricot Mold

Make 3 or 4 days ahead—unmold, place on lettuce leaves early New Year's Eve day, top with dressing and cherries, and refrigerate. You're ready for that late night evening!
Makes 10 individual molds or one 1½ quart mold
(See rule for congealing salads, p. 229)

1 6 ounce package apricot jello
1 cup orange juice
1 15 ounce can crushed pineapple, drained
1 16 oz. can apricot halves, drained

1 cup broken pecan pieces
2 cups buttermilk
1 6 oz. bottle green Maraschino cherries

1. Spray salad molds with a "no stick" cooking spray.
2. Heat orange juice in a small sauce pan until hot. Or microwave in a glass container for 2-2½ minutes on HIGH.
3. Add jello to orange juice and stir until dissolved. If not completely dissolved, reheat, stirring, until jello is completely dissolved. Set aside.
4. Cut one can of drained apricot halves in fourths. Pat dry with paper towel. Add to orange juice-jello mixture.
5. Stir in well drained crushed pineapple and nuts.
6. Add 2 cups buttermilk and stir to mix well.
7. Pour into molds and chill until firm.
8. To serve, unmold on bed of lettuce, top with cream cheese dressing and a green Maraschino cherry.

Cream Cheese Dressing

Make ahead–keeps well for 3-4 weeks
Makes 1 cup

**1 3 oz. package cream
cheese, softened**
**½ cup mayonnaise
(no substitutes)**
1 T. milk

**⅛ t. salt (or more if
desired)**
**1 t. bottled lemon juice
(optional)**

1. Mix cream cheese, mayonnaise, and milk together until well blended.
2. Add salt and lemon juice. Beat by hand until light and fluffy.
3. Cover and refrigerate until ready to serve.

Ginger Bread Raisin Muffins

Freezes well
Makes 21 muffins

**1 box Betty Crocker
Gingerbread Mix**
1¼ cups lukewarm water
1 egg

**2 1½ oz. boxes seedless
raisins**
paper muffin liners

1. Preheat oven to 350 degrees.
2. Combine gingerbread mix, lukewarm water, and egg.
3. Stir until ingredients are well combined.
4. Stir in raisins.
5. Place paper muffin liners in muffin tin.
6. Fill each container half full.
7. Bake 350 degrees for 20 minutes or until center comes out clean when tested with a toothpick.

Note: If frozen, let muffins come to room temperature, wrap in foil, and reheat in 300 degree oven approximately 15 minutes to serve warm.

Menu III

Fancy Egg Scramble

with

Broccoli and Ham

Spiced Peach Halves

Blueberry Muffins

Hot Coffee

Fancy Egg Scramble

A dish that can be prepared 24 hours in advance!
Left-overs reheat well
Serves 8

12 slices white bread, crusts removed and torn into pieces
1 10 oz. package frozen chopped broccoli, thawed and well drained
2 cups cooked ham, cubed
3 cups grated sharp Cheddar cheese
3 cups milk

12 eggs, slightly beaten
¼ cup chopped green onion tops
¼ t. dry mustard
⅛ t. Tabasco
1 t. Worcestershire
⅛ t. coarsely ground black pepper
¼-½ t. salt depending on taste

1. Preheat oven to 325 degrees if baking immediately.
2. Lightly grease a 8 x 12 inch baking dish or spray with "no stick" cooking spray.
3. Remove crusts from bread and tear into ½ inch pieces.
4. Mix together: eggs, milk, onion tops, dry mustard, Tabasco, Worcestershire, pepper, and salt. Whisk until well blended.
5. Layer as follows: place one half of bread cubes in bottom of baking dish; spread one half of cubed ham and one half of broccoli over top of bread cubes; top with 1 ½ cups grated Cheddar. Repeat layers ending up with cheese on top.
6. Pour milk/egg mixture over all. Cover tightly and refrigerate until ready to bake. Let come to room temperature before baking.
7. Bake 55 to 60 minutes at 325 degrees. Let sit 5 minutes before cutting into squares.

Spiced Peaches

Make 2-3 days ahead
Serves 6

**1 29 oz. can yellow cling
peach halves (buy a well
known brand)**
**¾ cup firmly packed
brown sugar**

½ cup cider vinegar
½ t. ground cloves
1 t. allspice
**1 t. whole cloves
(about 32)**

1. Drain peach juice through a small colander into a 2 quart sauce pan. Set peaches aside.
2. To saucepan add: brown sugar, vinegar, cloves, allspice, and whole cloves.
3. Bring to a boil and cook 5 minutes.
4. Reduce heat to medium low. Add peach halves and simmer 5 minutes.
5. Pour peach halves and syrup into a container and refrigerate for at least 24 hours. Drain before serving.

Blueberry Muffins

Make ahead of time. Freezes well.
Makes 24 individual muffins

2 13 oz. boxes blueberry muffin mix with "real" blueberries

1 16 oz. can blueberries, drained

1. Preheat oven to 400 degrees.
2. Drain well blueberries in box mix along with additional 16 oz. can blueberries.
3. In mixing bowl, blend 2 eggs and 1 cup milk.
4. Add muffin mix and stir until just moistened.
5. Fold in blueberries.
6. Fill well greased muffin tins or paper muffin cups ½ full.
7. Bake 400 degrees until light golden brown—approximately 15-20 minutes.

IF FROZEN, LET COME TO ROOM TEMPERATURE,
WRAP IN FOIL, AND HEAT IN A 300 DEGREE
OVEN FOR 10 MINUTES.

Note: If you prefer another type of muffin, avail yourself of the wide variety of mixes offered on the grocery shelf—or buy fresh breakfast pastries from your local bakery.

NEW YEAR'S DAY

Winning Menus for the Football Games!
Black-Eyed Peas for a Year of Good Luck!

NEW YEAR'S DAY

Football and Black-Eyed Peas

APPETIZERS FOR THE FOOTBALL FANS
Prepare Ahead and Enjoy the Guests!

Depending upon the time of day food is to be served, choose among the hearty appetizers pages 126-129, or suggestions for nibbling page 122. For a cheese and fruit board, see pages 32-34. For a tray of fresh vegetables and easy dips, see pages 40-42.

Menu I . . . . p. 147

Black-Eyed Peas
Carolina Brunswick Stew
Toasted Cornbread Squares
Red Christmas Aspic in Avocado Shells (optional)
Luscious Lemon Pie

Menu II . . . . p. 153

Marinated Black-Eyed Peas
Ten Minute Chili
Shredded Sharp Cheese and Minced Onions
Celebration Slaw
Dessert

Menu III. . . . . p. 158

New Year's Day Good Luck Buffet
Take Your Choice of Soups
New Year's Day Black-Eyed Pea Soup
Spicey Memphis Style Bean Soup
Sandwich and Salad Bar
Assorted Cheeses
Dessert

Menu 1

Black-Eyed Peas

Brunswick Stew

Toasted Cornbread Squares

Red Christmas Aspic in Avocado

Shells (optional)

Iced Mugs of Cold Beer

Ten Minute Luscious Lemon Pie

Coffee

Black-Eyed Peas
Serves 8-10

1 package of Artificial Ham
  Flavored
  Black-eyed Peas
  (A new product packed
  by N. K. Hurst Co.,
  Indianapolis, Ind.)
6 cups boiling water
1 onion (coarsely chopped)

1 t. light salt
½ t. black pepper
Contents of Artificial
  Ham flavoring

1. Rinse peas and drain.
2. Put 6 cups water on to boil.
3. Add peas, chopped onions, salt, and pepper
4. Simmer for 1½ hours, adding additional water if necessary. Stir off and on to prevent scorching.
5. During last hour add Contents of Artificial Ham Flavoring.

Carolina Brunswick Stew

One of the most popular and famous of all Southern dishes, every state claiming its origin, early recipes calling for squirrels instead of chicken.
A perfect main dish that can wait, flavor improving if left to stand overnight or frozen and re-heated.

Serves 8

Carolina Brunswick Stew

PART I

1 large plump hen
(approximately 5
pounds) or 2 broilers or
fryers (fat on chicken
adds flavor to the
broth and is skimmed
off later)
2 cups chopped onions–
1½-2 inch chunks
2 T. Hormel's Homestyle
Bacon Freeze, dried

¼ t. Tabasco
¼ t. coarsely ground black
pepper
½ t. light salt
1 T. sugar
4 T. Real Lemon
Concentrate
1 t. Worcestershire
10 cups water

PART II

8 cups broth
1 16 oz. package frozen
baby lima beans
1 heaping cup freshly
chopped white onion
1 24 oz. can all natural
peeled tomatoes

1 16 oz. package corn,
frozen (do not use
canned corn)
chicken–approximately
6 cups cut up
2 t. salt
1 t. coarsely ground black
pepper

PART I

1. In a large roaster or soup kettle, put one hen or two
   chickens, chopped onions, and all seasonings. Cover with
   10 cups water.
2. Bring to a boil. Reduce heat to medium low and simmer
   covered, 2 to 2½ hours or until meat can easily be
   removed from the bone. Stir occasionally.
3. Remove chicken to a platter and let cool
4. Strain broth, discarding everything but liquid. set in freezer
   or refrigerate and let fat rise to top. Remove fat with a
   spatula or lift with a knife and discard.
5. Cut chicken into small pieces (not diced). Discard all skin
   and any fat. Set aside.

Continued on next page

PART II

1. In same roaster or soup kettle, put 8 cups rich, strained broth. If you do not have adequate amount of broth to make 8 cups, add 1 14 oz. can Swanson's Chicken Broth or amount it takes to equal 8 cups.
2. Add onions, lima beans, tomatoes, salt and pepper. Bring to a boil, stir, and reduce heat to medium low. Let cook 20-25 minutes or until lima beans are tender.
3. Add chicken and corn and simmer slowly about 10 minutes.
4. If stew is too thin, put 1 T. flour in small mixing bowl. Add ½ to ¾ cup hot stock and whisk until well blended. Add to stew and stir to mix well. Simmer 2 to 3 minutes until it thickens.
5. Keep stew warm on top of stove or on an electric hot plate and let guests help themselves when they get hungry. Serve with toasted cornbread squares and red Christmas aspic in avacado shells.

Note: If stew is to be frozen, slightly undercook vegetables and do not add corn until heating to serve.

TOASTED CORNBREAD SQUARES

see page 19 for recipe

Red Christmas Aspic in Avocado Shells

Aspic can be made ahead and frozen or kept in
refrigerator for a week
See page 229 for congealing salads
½ ripe avocado for each invited guest*
Serves 18-20

**1 24 oz. bottle Mr. and Mrs.
T. or any good Bloody
Mary mix
2 T. unflavored gelatin
½ T. Worcestershire sauce**

**2 T. bottled lemon juice
½ t. bottled onion juice
⅛ t. sugar
Scant ⅛ t. ground cloves**

1. Dissolve gelatin in 1 cup Bloody Mary mix.
2. Combine remainder of Bloody Mary mix with
   Worcestershire sauce, lemon juice, onion juice, sugar, and
   cloves in uncovered saucepan. Bring to a boil.
3. Stir gelatin into hot mixture. Mix well, reduce heat, and
   simmer 5 minutes.
4. Pour hot mixture into 9 x 13 baking dish.
5. Refrigerate until firm.
6. Just before party time, cut avocados in half, discard seed.
7. Scoop a spoonful of aspic into each avocado half and
   garnish with parsley.
8. Cover tightly with plastic wrap and refrigerate until ready to
   serve.

CHOOSING AVOCADOS: Avocados should give just a little
bit to gentle pressure. Do not pinch as they bruise easily. If
bought when hard, put in paper sack and place in dark closet
or cupboard for fast ripening.

10-Minute Luscious Lemon Pie

Make ahead—keeps well for 3-4 days
Serves 6

**1 can sweetened
  condensed milk**
**½ cup lemon juice
  (approximately 3
  whole lemons)**
grated rind of 1 lemon

**1 6 oz. Ready Crust pie
  shell, graham cracker
  flavored**
**2 cups whipped topping
  with Real cream**

1. Grate lemon rind into mixing bowl.
2. Squeeze lemons and combine juice with rind and
   sweetened condensed milk.
3. Beat with whisk until all ingredients are well blended.
4. Spoon into graham cracker crust and refrigerate until filling
   is firm.
5. When firm, top with 2 cups whipped topping.

**Note: For that extra touch, garnish with thin slices of
       lemon**

Menu II

Marinated Black-Eyed Peas

Ten Minute Chili

Shredded Sharp Cheese and Minced Onions

Crackers or Corn Chips

Celebration Slaw

Iced Mugs of Cold Beer

Assortment of Cookies and Candy

Coffee

Marinated Black-Eyed Peas

Make ahead–keeps well for 3 weeks
Make 65 individual servings

1 16 oz. package
   black-eyed peas
1 t. salt
⅔ cup corn oil
¼ cup plus 1½ T. red
   wine vinegar
¼ cup dried chopped onion
   or 1 cup chopped onion
1 cup chopped fresh
   parsley (see rule, p 42,
   "How to Chop
   Parsley Easily")

2 garlic cloves crushed
   or pressed
2 t. dried basil
1 t. oregano
½ t. dry mustard
½ t. salt
½ t. coarsely ground black
   pepper
¾ t. Tabasco
Green pepper rings for
   garnish (optional)
crackers

1. Rinse peas and place in 2 quart sauce pan. Cover with water 2 inches over peas. Soak for 8 hours. Drain.

2. Return peas to pan, add salt, and cover with water. Bring to a boil, reduce heat to medium low, and simmer for 30-45 minutes. Cook until peas are tender. Drain. Combine oil and next 9 ingredients. Whisk to blend well. Put peas in serving dish, pour oil/vinegar combination over, and toss gently to coat. Taste. Add salt if needed. Cover tightly with plastic wrap and chill. Let come to room temperature before serving.

4. Garnish with green pepper strips (optional) and serve with Triscuits or bacon flavored crackers.

Ten Minute Chili

Make way ahead–takes only ten minutes to prepare
Freezes well
Serves 4 heartily
(Double and triple for amount of guests to be served)

**1 pound lean ground beef
(lean chuck preferred)
1 16 oz. can tomato sauce
1 15 oz. can chili beans,
Mexican style
1 15 oz. can kidney or pinto
beans
2 T. instant dried minced
onion
1 package chili seasoning
that calls for 2 pounds
meat per seasoning
package (Williams
preferred)**

**⅓ cup water
½ t. salt
⅛ t. coarsely ground black
pepper
1 clove garlic pressed or
finely minced**

1. In a 2 quart sauce pan or large skillet, brown beef. Drain well if needed.
2. Return drained beef to pan and add: tomato sauce, chili beans, kidney beans, minced onion, chili seasoning, water, salt, pepper, and garlic.
3. Bring to a boil, reduce heat to simmer, cover, and cook 15 minutes, stirring occasionally.
4. Uncover at end of 15 minutes and continue cooking 5 to 10 minutes or until liquid is reduced and chili is right consistency.
5. Pour into large serving bowl, keep warm, and serve with condiments.

Note: If chili has been frozen and is too thick when reheated, add a bit of water until it reaches correct consistency.

Condiments for Chili

Serves 4

1 medium onion
Saltines or corn chips

1 cup grated sharp
Cheddar cheese

1. Mince finely 1 medium onion. Place in small serving bowl.
2. Place 1 cup grated sharp Cheddar cheese in another small serving bowl.
3. Put saltines or corn chips in wooden or wicker basket beside bowls of cheese and onion.
4. Let guests help themselves to chili and condiments.

Celebration Slaw

Prepare ahead! The longer it stands, the better it tastes!
(Keeps up to three weeks)
Serves 10-12

Slaw

1 large head cabbage
1 green pepper

1 small onion
2 carrots

Dressing

1 cup sugar
1 t. salt
1 t. dry mustard

1 t. celery seed
1 cup corn or safflower oil
1 cup cider vinegar

1. Shred cabbage, green pepper, onion, and carrots.
2. Toss in a large bowl and set aside.
3. In a saucepan combine sugar, salt, mustard, celery seed, oil, and vinegar.
4. Bring to a boil, reduce heat to medium and cook 5 minutes. Cool slightly.
5. Pour over slaw, mixing well.
6. Cover and refrigerate.

Note: Without a fast method to shred cabbage, buy preshredded cabbage from the grocery.

To Shred in Blender: Cut 1 head of cabbage into very small sections. Put ¼ of cut cabbage into blender and fill to top with water. Push chop button and let run 2-3 seconds or until cabbage is coarsely chopped. Pour into colander and drain. Repeat. CAUTION: Be sure cabbage in WELL DRAINED before adding dressing.

Assortment of Cookies and Candy

See pages 167-174 and pages 189-195 for a tasty assortment of "make ahead and freeze" cookies and candy. Arrange attractively on a tray, garnish with sprigs of holly, and let the guests enjoy!

Menu III

Welcome the New Year with a "serve yourself" soup and sandwich bar straight from the cook's own kitchen...hearty and easy soups, made ahead and frozen; a tempting assortment of sandwich and salad accompaniments.

Choice of Four Soups

New Year's Day Black-Eyed Pea Soup

Spicey Memphis Style Bean Soup

New England Clam Chowder

Dilled Potato Soup

Assorted Sliced Meats

Pita Pockets

Salad Greens and Accompaniments

Assortment of Cheeses

Iced Beer and Soft Drinks

A Pie?... Cookies?... a Cake?

On the Counter

Colorful and durable dinner size paper
plates and matching napkins,

Salad forks and soup spoons

Serving forks and spoons

Earthenware or paper bowls for sandwich
and salad accompaniments

Wicker basket for pita pockets

Large glass bowl or tray of chilled, crisp and
torn greens

An inviting variety of bottled salad dressings
and sandwich spreads

An assortment of cheeses

Dessert

A pot of coffee

(and close by—a tub of iced beer
and soft drinks)

Good Luck Black-Eyed Pea Soup

Men love it!
Make ahead–Freezes well
Makes 12 one cup servings

1 pound black-eyed peas
6 slices bacon
2 cups chopped onion
(approximately 1 onion
weighing ½ pound)
vegetable oil (if needed)
1 T. All Purpose flour
1 14½ oz. can undrained
whole tomatoes
(Contadina preferred)
2 cloves garlic, pressed or
finely minced

1 t. Worcestershire sauce
¼ t. Tabasco
1½ t. salt
½ t. coarsely ground black
pepper
1 t. Knorr Swiss Aromat all-
purpose Seasoning
(optional-add more salt if
not using)
1 T. white wine vinegar
(optional, but adds zest)
1½ t. liquid smoke

1. Rinse peas. Place in large soup kettle and cover with water. Place lid on kettle and bring to a boil, reduce heat to medium, and simmer 2 minutes. Set aside, tightly covered for a minimum of one hour–can leave for 3-4 hours.
2. Drain peas in a colander and set aside.
3. Fry bacon in soup kettle until crisp. Drain, crumble and set aside.
4. Saute onions in bacon drippings until tender–2-3 minutes. Remove from pan and drain on paper towel.
5. Add enough oil to bacon drippings to make 2 T. Stir in 1 T. flour and whisk to blend well.
6. Add undrained tomatoes, garlic, Worcestershire, Tabasco, salt, pepper, Swiss Aromat Seasoning, white wine vinegar, liquid smoke, crumbled bacon, onions, and drained peas. Stir to mix well.

Continued on next page

7. Bring to a boil, reduce heat to simmer, and cook for 1-2 hours stirring occasionally. If peas have been left covered in water for over 2 hours, cooking time will be 45 minutes to 1 hour. If left for only an hour, cooking time will be 2-2½ hours. Cook until peas are tender.

8. Taste—add more salt if needed (black-eyed peas are very bland and require extra seasoning) and an additional ½ t. liquid smoke if desired.

9. Freeze in airtight containers. Serve hot in warm soup bowls.

Spicy Memphis Style Bean Soup

Hearty and delicious
(Can be made ahead and frozen)
Serves 8-10

1 lb. ground beef	**2 16 oz. cans Pinto Beans**
2 medium onions, sliced thin	**2 16 oz. cans tomatoes, undrained**
2 lb. head of cabbage cut into 2 inch chunks	**1 t. light salt**
1 cup chopped celery	**¼ t. black pepper**
	2 cups cold water

1. In medium size sauce pan brown beef and onions. Drain.

2. Add remaining ingredients.

3. Simmer approximately 30-45 minutes.

4. Taste for flavor and serve. Or put in airtight containers and freeze.

New England Clam Chowder

So easy and quick you won't believe the delectable taste!
Make ahead–Freezes well
Makes 7 one cup servings

2 6½ oz. cans minced
clams
2 15 oz. cans Snow's Clam
Chowder
1 14½ can Swanson's
Chicken Broth
1 t. minced dried chives

⅔ Half and Half or whole
milk
⅛ t. Tabasco
1 t. dried parsley flakes
¼ t. coarsely ground black
pepper
1½ T. sherry

1. Drain clam liquid into soup pot. Set clams aside.
2. In same soup pot, add 2 cans clam chowder, chicken broth, 1 t. minced chives, ¾ cup Half and Half, ⅛ t. Tabasco, 1 t. dried parsley flakes, and ¼ t. pepper.
3. Bring to a boil, reduce heat, and simmer 5 minutes, stirring constantly.
4. Add clams and sherry. Stir to mix well and let sit five minutes for flavors to blend.
5. Pour into airtight containers or jars if freezing or holding in refrigerator.

Dilled Potato Soup

Delicious and ready in 10 minutes!
Makes 6 ½ cup servings

1 10¾ oz. can Cream of
Potato soup
1 soup can milk
dash white pepper

⅛ t. salt
1 t. dried dill
⅔ cup sour cream or "lite"
sour cream

1. Mix soup, milk, pepper, salt, and dill in soup pan.
2. Heat until hot, stirring constantly with wire whisk.
3. Stir in sour cream.
4. Pour into soup bowls and sprinkle with paprika for color.

Salad and Sandwich Bar

Make a light salad or a hearty sandwich
Guests choose from the following variety
of choices offered
Serves 8-10

corned beef, thinly sliced*
smoked turkey, thinly
  sliced*
ham, thinly sliced*
salami or pastrami,
  thinly sliced*
rare roast beef, thinly
  sliced*
1 head iceberg lettuce
1 bunch Romaine lettuce
½ pound fresh bean
  sprouts
2 green peppers, diced
1 head fresh cauliflower
  (flowerettes only)
1 head fresh broccoli
  (flowerettes only)

½ pound fresh
  mushrooms, sliced
2 cucumbers seeded
  and diced
1 -2 sweet, red onions,
  sliced
1 8 ounce can seedless ripe
  olives drained
2 -3 hard cooked eggs,
  chopped
1 jar bacon bits
1 box of salad croutons
Pita Pockets–amount
  needed depends upon
  number of invited guests

*Choose minimum of two meats and allow ⅛ pound meat per
person

CHEESE SELECTIONS

1 8 oz. block sharp Cheddar   1 6 ounce round Bleu
1 10 oz. rectangle Munster
  or Monterey Jack

DRESSING SELECTIONS

Mayonnaise
Mustard (Dijon or brand
  equally tasty)
Bleu Cheese Salad
  Dressing (store bought)

Oil and Vinegar (store
  bought)
Thousand Island or French
  (store bought)

Continued on next page

THE DAY BEFORE

1. Cut ends off pita pockets. Place on serving tray and cover tightly until ready to serve.
2. Wash lettuce and drain well. Wrap in paper toweling or dish towel, put in air-tight plastic bag, and refrigerate until ready to use.
3. At serving time, or earlier in day, tear lettuce into approximately 2½ to 3 inch pieces and place in large glass bowl.
4. Wash all vegetables and drain well. Slice or dice into bite sized pieces. Cover tightly in individual serving bowls and refrigerate until ready to serve.
5. Arrange meat attractively on large serving platter. Cover tightly with aluminum foil or plastic wrap. Garnish with parsley or curly endive before serving.

Note: Keep all salad greens and accompaniments well chilled until party time, except cheese. Prepare cheese tray ahead of time and let come to room temperature for full flavor.

Dessert

The grand finale can be the effortless selection of irresistible desserts from the grocery frozen food section.
Or select from the variety of desserts, pages 167-198 that can be made ahead and frozen.

SWEET FINALES!
A TREASURY OF CHRISTMAS DESSERTS

From Generation to Generation...the Best of the Best

SWEET FINALES!
A TREASURY OF CHRISTMAS DESSERTS

COOKIES

Melt In Your Mouth Chocolate Cocoanut Macaroons

(Everybody's favorite)
Freezes well
Yields 50 to 55 cookies

**1 cup sweetened
  condensed milk
4 cups cocoanut
⅔ cup mini semi sweet
  chocolate bits**

**1 t. vanilla extract
½ t. almond extract**

1. Preheat oven to 325 degrees.
2. Combine sweetened condensed milk and cocoanut. Mix well by hand–mixture will be gooey.
3. Add chocolate bits, vanilla, and almond. Stir until all ingredients are well blended.
4. Lightly spray a "non stick" (Teflon coated) cookie sheet with a "no stick" cooking spray.
5. Drop by teaspoonfuls onto cookie sheet, one inch apart.
6. Cook 12 minutes or until lightly brown on top.
7. Remove from pan with a teflon coated spatula and let cool.
8. Store in an airtight container or in ziploc freezer bags.

Dreamy Date Balls

The best of the tried and true date balls
Freezes well–keeps for a week to 10 days
Yields 36 to 40 balls

**1 stick butter or butter
  substitute**
1 cup sugar
**1 8 ounce box chopped
  dates**

1 cup Rice Crispies
1 cup chopped pecans
1 t. vanilla extract
powdered sugar

1. In a 2 quart saucepan, combine butter, sugar, and chopped dates.
2. Heat on medium low, stirring, until all ingredients are melted and well blended.
3. Remove from heat. Add Rice Crispies, chopped pecans, and vanilla. Stir to mix well.
4. Roll into balls about one half inch in diameter.
5. Drop balls, a few at a time, into a small grocery store sack or a plastic bag with enough powdered sugar to cover. Shake lightly until date balls are coated with sugar.
6. Place in an airtight container or freezer ziploc bag. Store at room temperature or freeze until ready to serve.

Cornflake Crinkles

A crisp, delicious cookie that can be made well ahead—
Freezes well
Yields 36 to 40 cookies

**1 cup butter (2 sticks) or
butter substitute,
room temperature
1 cup sugar
1½ cups pre sifted, all
purpose flour**

**1 t. vanilla extract
½ t. salt
1 t. cream of tartar
1 t. baking soda
4 cups cornflakes
1 cup chopped pecans**

1. Preheat oven to 300 degrees.
2. In a large bowl, combine butter and sugar and beat until creamy and smooth.
3. Gradually add flour, vanilla, salt, cream of tartar, and soda. Beat until mixture is smooth and ingredients are well blended.
4. Fold in cornflakes and pecans—DO NOT CRUSH CORNFLAKES.
5. Drop by teaspoonfuls onto an ungreased cookie sheet.
6. Bake 300 degrees 12 to 15 minutes or until slightly brown. Store in tightly covered cookie tin or ziploc bag.

Sugared Sand Tarts

What would Christmas be without these crunchy rich morsels to nibble on?
A traditional favorite in our house

Freezes beautifully–keeps well for a week to 10 days
Yields 5-6 dozen 2 inch cookies

2 cups sugar
1 cup butter (2 sticks) or
butter substitute,
room temperature
2 eggs (omit one white and
set aside)

3 cups all purpose flour
1 t. baking soda
2 t. cream of tartar
Cinnamon sugar to sprinkle
on top

1. Preheat oven to 350 degrees.
2. Combine sugar, butter, and eggs. Beat until creamy and smooth.
3. Mix together flour, soda, and cream of tartar. Add gradually to sugar/butter mixture, mixing well after each addition.
4. Form dough into rolls approximately 12 inches long and 2 inches in diameter. Dough may be a bit crumbly, but will be fine after refrigeration. Wrap in wax paper or aluminum foil and refrigerate at least 1 hour or until ready to bake. NOTE– Dough can be wrapped for freezer at this point and frozen up to two months.
5. Remove one roll from refrigerator at a time. Slice ⅛ inch thick and place on greased cookie sheet or a "no stick" Teflon coated cookie sheet.
6. Brush top of each cookie with egg white and sprinkle with cinnamon sugar.
7. Bake 9-10 minutes until light brown.
8. Remove from pan, let cool, and place in air tight containers or ziploc freezer bags. Freezes well for up to three months if kept in air tight container.

Swedish Butter Cookies

A delight to the eye!
Freezes well
Yields 3½ dozen

½ cup butter (1 stick) or butter substitute, room temperature
¼ cup sugar
1 egg yolk slightly beaten
1 cup all purpose flour, pre sifted

1 t. vanilla extract
½ t. almond extract
¾ cup nut meats finely chopped (preferably pecans, but can use toasted almonds or walnuts)

1. Preheat oven to 300 degrees.
2. Combine butter, sugar, and egg yolk. Beat until creamy and smooth.
3. Gradually add flour, vanilla, almond, and nut meats, beating until all ingredients are well blended.
4. Form into small balls about ½ inch in diameter.
5. Place on a "non stick" cookie sheet and press lightly with a fork for waffle effect (Dip fork into cold water if it becomes sticky)
6. Bake 5 minutes and remove from oven.
7. With your finger, press center of each cookie down to form a small indentation. Return to oven and cook for 15 minutes or until golden brown.
8. Remove from oven, let cool, and fill centers with a tart jam.
9. Store in airtight container. If cookies are to be frozen, do not fill with jam until thawed out. If cookie is soft when thawed, place in a 300 degree oven for 5 minutes to restore crispness.

Christmas Cut Outs

That special sugar cookie children love to cut out, and adults find equally delectable to nibble on—even if the Santa doesn't resemble Jolly 'ole Saint Nick after little Johnny has made his mark!

Makes approximately 5 dozen cookies

USE A NON STICK (TEFLON COATED) COOKIE PAN
DO NOT GREASE OR COOKIES WILL SPREAD AND LOSE
THEIR SHAPE

6 T. butter or butter substitute, room temperature
1 cup sugar
2 eggs
1 t. vanilla extract

2½ cups all purpose flour
1 t. baking powder
1 t. salt
powdered sugar for rolling dough

1. Preheat oven to 400 degrees.
2. In a large mixing bowl, combine butter, sugar, eggs, and vanilla. Beat until well blended and light and fluffy.
3. Add flour, baking powder, and salt. Beat until all ingredients are well mixed.
4. Cover and chill dough in refrigerator one hour.
5. Sprinkle powdered sugar on counter or cookie sheet (cookies will not toughen as they are likely to do when rolled in flour).
6. Roll dough ⅛ inch thick and cut into desired shapes. (Roll dough directly on cookie sheet, cut into shapes, and remove dough in between cut outs—saves transferring cookies which is sometimes difficult).
7. Bake 6 to 8 minutes at 400 degrees.
8. Remove immediately from cookie sheet and let cool before decorating.

Ornamental Icings for Christmas Cut Outs

There is a wide variety of decorative icings and gels already available on the grocery shelves. Many are already in the tube so that even the smallest of children can quickly become an artist. Use your imagination—buy an assortment of red and green sugars, silver dragees, chocolate shavings, cinnamon bits, raisins, etc. to add the final flourish to any cookie.

ICING MIXES FROM THE BOX

Use prepared vanilla frosting and tint any color you wish. Follow package directions, but reduce water by 4 teaspoons to make a stiffer consistency which is better for decorative icings.

CANNED ICINGS

Any canned icing may be used. If it becomes too soft while decorating, refrigerate until it acquires a stiff consistency

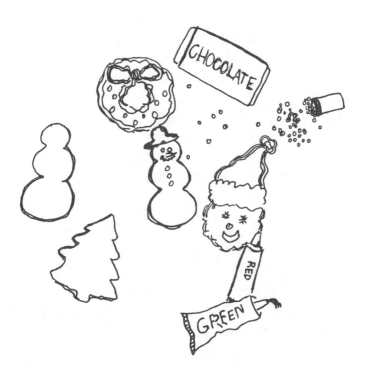

Scrumptious Chocolate Surprises

Make ahead and freeze
Yields 6 dozen

1¼ cups (1½ sticks)
  butter or butter
  substitute, room
  temperature
2 cups sugar
2 eggs

2 t. vanilla extract
¾ cup unsweetened cocoa
  powder
2 cups all purpose flour
1 t. baking soda
1 t. salt

Topping

1 10 oz. bag large
  marshmallows

1 6 oz. bag semi sweet
  chocolate chips

1. Preheat oven to 350 degrees.
2. In a large bowl, cream butter, sugar, eggs, and vanilla.
3. Add cocoa and mix until well blended.
4. Add flour, soda, and salt. This mixture will seem very thick. Mix until well blended.
5. Drop by one half teaspoonfuls on a greased cookie sheet–or use a Teflon, no stick cookie sheet.
6. Bake 8 minutes at 350 degrees.
7. While cookies are baking, quarter marshmallows and set aside. Dip scissors into cold water if they become sticky.
8. Remove cookies from oven at 8 minutes, top each cookie with one quarter of a marshmallow and return to oven.
9. Cook 4 minutes. Remove from oven and place one semi sweet chocolate chip in center of each marshmallow. Gently press chocolate chip into marshmallow. Heat from cookie will slightly melt bottom of chip and allow chocolate chip to adhere to marshmallow.
10. Let cool completely and store in an airtight container, or freeze up to 2 months.

Donna's Short-Cut Old Fashioned Fruit Cake

Puffed with Fruit and Soaked in Spirits
Keeps 3-4 months in refrigerator
Serves 18-20 or more depending upon size sliced

PART I

**3 cups raisins
(1 8 oz. box)
2 cups hot water**

**½ cup shortening
2 cups sugar
1 cup cold water**

PART II

**4 cups all purpose flour, pre
sifted
1 T. baking soda**

**1 t. salt
½ t. cinnamon**

PART III

**1½ pound mixed fruit
1 8 oz. container whole
candied cherries
1½ cups whole pecan
halves**

**1½ cups whole English
walnuts
1 cup brandy or dry sherry**

PART I

1. Preheat oven to 350 degrees.
2. Grease and flour a 9″ tube pan or 3 to 4 loaf pans.
3. Put 2 cups water on to boil. Reduce heat to a medium boil and add 3 cups raisins. Boil for 15 minutes. At end of 15 minutes, water will almost be boiled out of raisins.
4. Reduce heat to low and add ½ cup shortening and 2 cups sugar. Stir until melted. Remove from heat.
5. Add 1 cup cold water. Stir and set aside to cool.

PART II

1. In a mixing bowl combine: flour, soda, salt and cinnamon. Stir to mix well.
2. Add cooled raisin mixture (PART I) to dry ingredients in Part II. Mix well until all ingredients are well blended.

Continued on next page

PART III

1. To cake batter, add fruit, pecan halves, and walnuts. Again, mix well until all ingredients are well blended.
2. Pour into tube pan or loaf pans and bake 1½ hours at 350 degrees. Test for doneness with toothpick or broom straw.* (If using loaf pans, fill ¾ full and check at 30 minutes)
3. Place cake open side up, and let cool.
4. When cold, turn out on piece of cloth big enough to wrap around cake.
5. Pour ½ cup brandy or sherry over top of cake and let drizzle down sides. After cake has absorbed brandy (or sherry) wrap in cloth and pour other half cup of brandy over.
6. Wrap tightly in heavy duty aluminum foil and refrigerate until ready to serve. Serve at room temperature. Will keep for 3-4 months in refrigerator, but pour another cup of brandy or sherry over cake in 2-3 weeks if not using immediately.

*TO TEST FOR DONENESS—insert a toothpick or a broom straw in center of cake—if filling adheres to toothpick or straw, cook longer. If toothpick comes out clean, cake is ready to be removed from oven.

Festive Layered Japanese Fruit Cake

A modern and easy version of an old fashioned favorite
Makes a beautiful 3 layer cake—Freezes well
Serves 20

1 Duncan Hines Traditions Spice Cake mix
1 3¾ ounce box vanilla pudding and pie filling mix
1 stick butter* or butter substitute, room temperature
1¼ cups water
4 eggs
1 cup cocoanut
1 cup raisins
.1 cup pecans pieces

1. Preheat oven to 350 degrees.
2. Grease and flour 3 nine inch cake pans.
3. In a mixing bowl combine cake mix, pudding mix, butter, water, and eggs. Mix until all ingredients are well blended.
4. Stir in cocoanut, raisins, and pecans.
5. Divide batter evenly among 3 nine inch cake pans.
6. Bake 35 minutes at 350 degrees. Test for doneness with toothpick or broomstraw. See page 176.
7. Remove from oven, cool in pans. Invert and turn out on wax paper when cool.

Frosting

1 cup orange pulp (approximately 3 small oranges)
¼ cup lemon pulp (approximately 2 medium lemons)

1½ cup hot water
2 cups sugar
4 T. flour
2½ cups cocoanut

1. Peel oranges and lemons with sharp knife, and throw away rinds. Cut up pulp finely including membranes of oranges and lemons.
2. Place in a 2 quart saucepan.
3. Mix flour with sugar, add to orange/lemon mixture.
4. Add 1½ cups hot water and bring to a boil. Reduce heat to medium and cook for about 20 minutes or until icing is right consistency. This will be fairly runny—do not cook until frosting looks like regular cake icing.
5. Let cool. Fold in cocoanut and spread between each cake layer and over sides.
6. Wrap in heavy aluminum foil and refrigerate or freeze.

Christmas Pound Cake

Make well ahead–keeps in freezer for 3 months
Keeps well unrefrigerated for a week to 10 days
Serves 18-20

**1 18.25 box yellow cake mix
(Betty Crocker Super
Moist Butter yellow cake
mix preferred)
1 3¾ box vanilla pudding
and pie filling mix**

**3 eggs
⅓ cup corn oil
¾ cup Apricot Nectar
(1 5½ oz. can)
¼ cup Apricot Brandy
1½ t. pure orange extract**

1. Preheat oven to 325 degrees.
2. Grease and flour a 10″ bundt pan (or any pan of equivalent size).
3. In mixing bowl combine cake mix, pudding mix, eggs, oil, Apricot Brandy, apricot nectar, and orange extract.
4. Mix until all ingredients are well blended.
5. Pour into bundt pan and cook 1 hour at 325 degrees or until cake tests done.
6. Invert on a cake plate and prick all over before spooning on glaze.

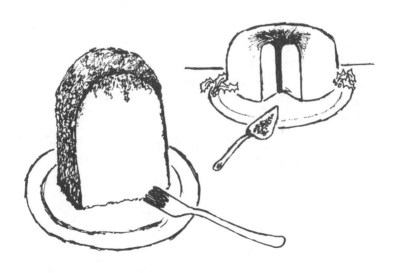

Glaze

4 T. butter
¾ cup sugar

⅓ cup Apricot Brandy
¼ cup water

1. Heat butter, sugar, and water in small saucepan until butter is melted and sugar is dissolved.
2. Remove from heat, add Apricot Brandy, mixing well.
3. Prick cake on top and sides with fork.
4. Spoon glaze slowly over cake, letting cake absorb liquid before adding additional glaze.
5. If freezing, wrap in heavy aluminum foil, leave out overnight. Wrap additionally in freezer wrap, tape all open edges closed, and freeze.

To Serve: Place on a cake platter, surround with fresh holly, place sprigs of fresh holly on top of cake, and tuck either red marachino or candied cherries in and among the holly leaves.

Colonial Tipsy Cake

"A MUST!"

An adaptation of English Trifle, it was known, also, as Tipsy Squire or Tipsy Parson—a special dessert to be served when the parson came to dine

Make ahead—give the sherry two or three days
to season the cake.
Freezes well
Yield—about 20 servings

Cake Ingredients

6 eggs, separated (reserve whites in separate bowl)
¾ cup sugar
1 t. vanilla extract
1½ cups all purpose flour, pre sifted

1½ t. baking powder
½ t. salt
4½ T. cold water
reserved egg white
¾ cup sugar for egg whites

Filling

1¼ cups sherry
1 cup apple jelly

1¼ cup sliced almonds toasted

Custard

4 cups milk
1½ cups sugar
¼ cup all purpose flour

⅛ t. salt
6 eggs, beaten
2 t. vanilla extract

Whipped Topping

1 16 oz. container whipped topping

1 t. vanilla extract

CAKE

1. Preheat oven to 350 degrees.
2. Beat egg yolks until light in color.
3. Gradually add ¾ cup sugar and vanilla, beating until thick and lemon colored.
4. Combine flour, baking powder, and salt. Add to egg mixture alternately with 4½ T. water, mixing well.
5. In a separate bowl, beat egg whites until foamy. Gradually add, beating constantly, ¾ cup sugar. Beat until stiff peaks form.
6. Fold egg whites into cake batter until thoroughtly mixed.
7. Pour cake batter into an ungreased 10″ tube pan.
8. Cook 25-30 minutes in a 350 degree oven. While cake is cooking, make custard. When cake is golden brown and begins to pull away from the side of the pan, test with a toothpick or broomstraw for doneness. Toothpick should be clean with no batter adhering to it when inserted into center of cake.
9. Invert pan on a cake rack or place knife handles underneath to prop up pan. Let cool completely before removing from pan.

CUSTARD

This recipe makes double the amount needed to spread on cake. Reserve half and pass at the table when serving cake–delicious accompaniment. If freezing cake, freeze extra custard in a separate container.

1. Spray bottom of two sauce pans with a "no stick" coating spray.
2. In one sauce pan, heat milk to almost boiling, but do not boil. Set aside, but keep warm.
3. In a 2 quart saucepan, combine sugar, flour, and salt. Add eggs and beat until well mixed.
4. Gradually add milk, stirring constantly until well blended.

Continued on next page

5. Place over medium heat and cook until mixture thickens and coats the spoon. Stir constantly, about 10 minutes.
6. Remove from heat and cool. Stir in vanilla. If custard is not smooth, process in a blender or strain through a sieve.
7. Set aside or refrigerate until ready to use.

ASSEMBLY OF CAKE

1. Split cake in two layers. Place one layer on cake platter and other on heavy aluminum foil or plate that will allow cake to slide off easily.
2. Drizzle ½ cup sherry over each layer. Divide remaining ¼ cup and drizzle over layers. OPTION–in by gone days, rule of thumb was to wrap Tipsy cake loosely with plastic wrap and let sit for one day to let sherry penetrate. If time does not allow for this procedure, continue with the following directions, but let cake sit, unwrapped, for at least an hour.
3. Spread bottom layer of cake with ½ cup apple jelly and sprinkle with ½ cup toasted almonds. Top with a layer of custard. Place other layer of cake on top and repeat layers of jelly, almonds, and custard. Reserve remaining ¼ cup almonds for top.
4. IF FREEZING–do not frost. Wrap cake tightly in aluminum foil or plastic wrap, then in freezer paper. Freeze until ready to serve.
5. If not freezing, it is better to wrap cake in plastic wrap and refrigerate for one day before icing. Cake can be served same day, but flavor is more delectable when allowed to sit for a day.

FROSTING

1. Add 1 t. vanilla to carton of whipped topping. Whisk or mix until well blended.
2. Spread over top and sides of cake. Sprinkle with remaining ¼ cup toasted almonds. Refrigerate until ready to serve.

Holiday Cocoanut Cake

Prepare ahead–freezes well
Serves 18-20

CAKE

1 18 ounce box Super-
moist yellow cake mix
with pudding in the mix
1 3½ oz. box vanilla
instant pudding and
pie filling mix
4 eggs

1⅓ cups water
½ cup corn oil
2 cups cocoanut, frozen,
fresh, or packaged
1 cup chopped pecans or
walnuts

Cocoanut Cream Cheese Frosting

4 T. butter or butter
substitute, room
temperature
2 cups cocoanut, fresh,
frozen, or packaged
1 8 oz. package cream
cheese, room
temperature

1 T. plus 1 t. milk
3 cups powdered sugar
½ t. vanilla

1. Preheat oven to 350 degrees.
2. Grease or spray with a "no stick" cooking spray 3 round 9"
   cake pans.
3. In a large mixing bowl, mix together until well blended:
   cake mix, pudding, eggs, water, corn oil.
4. Stir in cocoanut and chopped nuts.
5. Distribute batter evenly among 3 cake pans. Bake 20-25
   minutes at 350 degrees. Test with a toothpick or broomstraw
   at end of 30 minutes. Toothpick should be clean with no
   batter adhering to it when inserted into center of cake.
6. Remove from oven and let cool in pans for 15 minutes.
   Invert pans on wax paper. Remove cake and frost
   when cool.

Continued on next page

Frosting

1. Melt 2 T. butter in a skillet on medium heat. Reduce heat to medium low, add 2 cups cocoanut and stir until lightly browned. Remove and spread on an absorbent paper towel. Set aside.
2. In a small mixing bowl, mix together 2 T. butter, cream cheese, milk, powdered sugar, and vanilla. Beat until well blended.
3. Add cocoanut, mixing to blend well.
4. Spread a small amount on first two layers. Top with third layer and spread frosting over top and sides.
5. Cover tightly with foil until ready to serve.

Cheese Cake Supreme

The best of all cheesecakes

Don't let the preparation time to beat cake scare you—put ingredients in mixer and let the mixer do the work

Make ahead—keeps in refrigerator for a week
to 10 days—freezes well
Serves 20-22

PART I

½ **box vanilla wafers**
½ **box zwiback**
¼ **cup (½ stick) butter or butter substitute, melted**

¼ **cup firmly packed brown sugar**
1 **t. cinnamon**

PART II

3 **8 oz. packages cream cheese or "lite cream cheese", room temperature**

4 **eggs**
1 **cup sugar**
1 **t. vanilla**

PART III

1 pint sour cream (2 8 oz. cartons) or "Lite Sour Cream"

½ cup sugar
1 t. vanilla

TOPPING

1 jar currant jelly
2 T. water

fresh strawberries or blueberries (optional)

PART I

1. In a food processor, grind vanilla wafers and zwiback until they are pulverized. No food processor? Put into a ziploc bag, seal closed, and pound with a hammer or blunt object until wafers and zwibach are pulverized.
2. Add melted butter, brown sugar, and cinnamon. Stir to mix well.
3. Pat firmly into bottom of 10″ spring form pan. Set aside.

PART II

1. Preheat oven to 325 degrees.
2. In a large mixing bowl, combine cream cheese, eggs, sugar, and vanilla.
3. Beat for 30 minutes.
4. Pour over crust and bake 1 hour to 1 hour 15 minutes at 325 degrees. Check at end of 1 hour.
5. Test for doneness in center with a toothpick or broom straw. Center should be set and toothpick should not have any batter on it.
6. Refrigerate to cool.

PART III

While cake is cooling, combine and beat the following for 20 minutes:

1. In a small mixing bowl, combine sour cream, sugar, and vanilla.

Continued on next page

2. Beat for 20 minutes. Let mixer do the work. You do not have to stand over this while beating.

3. *Remove cooled cheesecake from refrigerator and spread with sour cream mixture.*

4. *Return to oven and bake 15 minutes at 325 degrees. Check for doneness. Center will be set and not wobbly. Top will not be brown.*

5. *Refrigerate until ready to spread topping. Spread topping next day if more convenient.*

Topping

1. Heat 1 jar currant jelly with 2 T. of water.

2. Decorate top with fresh strawberries or blueberries–optional.

3. Lightly drizzle jelly mixture over top and sides of cheesecake, being careful to spoon over strawberries or blueberries also.

4. Refrigerate until ready to serve.

5. At serving time, surround base with holly and place a few sprigs of holly on top of cake.

Chocolate Amaretto Cheesecake

The MOST fabulous of desserts!
Make ahead and freeze–keeps well in refrigerator
7-10 days
Serves 20-22

PART I

½ **box vanilla wafers**
½ **box zwibach**
¼ **cup melted butter**
   (½ stick)

¼ **cup firmly packed**
   brown sugar
½ **t. almond extract**

PART II

3 8 oz. packages cream
  cheese or "lite cream
  cheese", room
  temperature
4 eggs
1 cup sugar

1 t. vanilla
5 T. (¼ cup plus 1 T.)
  Amaretto (see page 189
  if you wish to make your
  own Amaretto)

PART III

1 pint sour cream
  (2 8 oz. cartons) or
  "lite sour cream"

½ cup sugar
1 t. vanilla

Topping

½ cup mini semi sweet
  chocolate bits
½ T. honey

2 T. butter
1 T. plus 1 t. Amaretto

1. In a food processor, grind vanilla wafers and zwibach until they are pulverized. No food processor? Put into a ziploc bag, seal closed, and pound with a hammer or blunt object until wafers and zwibach are pulverized.
2. Add melted butter, brown sugar, and almond extract. Stir to mix well.
3. Pat firmly into bottom of 10″ spring form pan. Set aside.

PART II

Even though this part requires beating for 30 minutes, let the mixer do the work. IT is not necessary to stir.

1. Preheat oven to 325 degrees.
2. In a large mixing bowl, combine cream cheese, eggs, sugar, vanilla, and Amaretto.
3. Beat on high for 30 minutes.
4. Pour over crust and bake 1 hour to 1 hour fifteen minutes at 325 degrees. Check at end of 1 hour.

Continued on next page

5. Test for doneness in center with a toothpick or broom straw. Center should be set and toothpick should not have any batter on it.
6. Remove from oven and refrigerate to cool.

PART III

While cake is cooling in refrigerator, combine and beat the following for 20 minutes

1. In a small mixing bowl, combine sour cream, sugar and vanilla.
2. Beat for 20 minutes on high. Let the mixer do the work. You do not have to stand over this while beating.
3. Remove cooled cheesecake from refrigerator and spread with sour cream mixture.
4. Return to oven and bake 15 minutes at 325 degrees. Check for doneness. Center should be set and not wobbly. Top will not be brown. Let cool.
5. Cheesecake may be frozen at this point or glazed with topping and frozen. Topping can also be dribbled on following day if desired. Refrigerate until ready to glaze or serve.

Topping

1. In a small sauce pan, melt ½ cup mini chocolate chips and ½ T. honey.
2. Stir until chocolate is melted—about 5 minutes.
3. Remove from heat, stir in 1 T. plus 1 t. Amaretto.
4. Dribble over top of cheesecake with an ice tea spoon.
5. Refrigerate or freeze until ready to serve.

To Decorate: place a few fresh holly sprigs on top of cake along with red and green marachino cherries. Surround base with holly.

Amaretto

If you do not wish to purchase Amaretto, the following recipe is a delicious rendition of the liqueur. MAKE IN ADVANCE TO ALLOW TIME TO SEASON.

Yields approximately 2 quarts

3 cups sugar
2¼ cups water
rind of 3 lemons
 finely graded

1 quart vodka
3 T. almond extract
2 T. vanilla extract (not
 imitation)

1. Combine sugar, water, and lemon rind in a large pan. Bring mixture to a boil. Reduce heat. Let simmer 5 minutes, stirring occasionally.
2. Remove from stove. Add vodka, almond, and vanilla. Stir to mix well.
3. Store in airtight jars.

Super Delectable Peanut Brittle

A three generation recipe
Keeps well in cool dry location for a month
Makes 2 pounds

2 cups sugar
1 cup white Karo syrup
2 cups boiling water
1 pound raw Spanish
 peanuts

3 scant t. baking soda
2 t. vanilla
2 T. butter or butter
 substitute

Continued on next page

1. Put baking soda in a custard cup or small dish and set aside.
2. Put vanilla and butter in another small dish and set aside.
3. Grease heavily with margarine a marble slab, kitchen counter, or a large cookie sheet.
4. In an electric frying pan or heavy 6 cup frying pan put 2 cups sugar, 1 cup Karo, and 2 cups boiling water. Use same cup for measuring. Boiling water will wash out remaining syrup from cup.
5. Cook on high, without stirring, for approximately 20 minutes or until it reaches the hard crack stage (300°-310° F) or cracks audibly to the ear. (Fill a small custard cup with ice water and drop a teaspoon of syrup in the water– if brittle is ready, you will hear an audible crack when it hits the cold water)
6. Immediately add raw peanuts and cook until they begin to turn beige, stirring occasionally. About 8-10 minutes.
7. Remove from heat and quickly add soda, vanilla, and butter. Stir vigorously until all ingredients are blended– only takes a minute.
8. Pour out on cold, buttered slab. Do not dump candy in one glob, but try to pour so candy will be as thin as possible.
9. Allow to stand for only a minute or until edges can be lifted with a buttered knife or spatula. Begin pulling immediately so brittle does not harden. (Note: Put on rubber gloves that have been rubbed with butter to pull–helps prevent burning)
10. Work toward the middle, pulling gently up and out. Pull until very thin.
11. Let cool completely and break into large pieces. Store in an air tight container in a cool, dry location. Keeps well for a month.

Suggestion: Freeze the crunchy leavings after the brittle has been broken and serve over vanilla ice cream–delicious!

Quick Microwave Peanut Brittle

Keeps well for a month stored in air tight container.
Store in cool dry location
Makes 1 pound

POWER LEVEL: HIGH
MICROWAVE TIME: 8-11 MINUTES
(Author's note: the old fashioned method makes
a thinner brittle–and with no stirring, it isn't
difficult or time consuming)

1 cup sugar	**1 t. butter**
½ cup white Karo syrup	**1 t. vanilla extract**
1 cup raw Spanish peanuts	**1 t. baking soda**

1. Put butter and vanilla in small bowl or custard cup and set aside.
2. Put soda in small cup and set aside.
3. Heavily grease with margarine a marble slab, kitchen counter, or large cookie sheet
4. In a 1½ quart glass casserole dish, stir together sugar and syrup until well mixed. Microwave on HIGH 4 minutes.
5. Stir in peanuts. Microwave on HIGH 3 to 5 minutes or until peanuts have turned light brown.
6. Add butter and vanilla to syrup, blending well. Microwave on HIGH 1 to 2 minutes. Remove from oven taking care not to spill–syrup will be very hot.
7. Quickly stir in soda and pour out on cold buttered slab. Try not to dump mixture in one thick glob, but pour so candy will be as thin as possible.
8. Follow directions on page 190 beginning with #9 for finishing brittle.

Chocolate Nut Fudge

Keeps well for a month in cool dry location
Makes 3 pounds

3 cups sugar
1½ sticks butter or
butter substitute
⅔ cup (5⅓ oz. can)
evaporated milk
1 12 oz. package Mini semi-
sweet chocolate bits

1 7 oz. jar Marshmallow
Creme
1 cup chopped pecans
or walnuts
1 t. vanilla

1. Grease a 13 x 9 inch glass baking pan.
2. Combine sugar, butter, and milk in a heavy 2 quart sauce pan.
3. Bring to a boil, *stirring constantly*.
4. Reduce heat to medium and stir constantly until mixture reaches a soft ball stage–about 7 to 12 minutes. Candy thermometer will read 235 degrees. If you have no candy thermometer, drop a teaspoonful of the liquid into a small amount of cold water. If it forms a soft ball, candy is ready– if runny and willl not form into a ball, continue cooking and retest after a few minutes.
5. Remove from stove and stir in chocolate bits and marshmallow creme. Stir vigorously until all ingredients are well blended and chocolate is melted.
6. Stir in vanilla and nuts.
7. Pour into a greased 13 x 9 inch pan and let cool. Cut into squares when cool. Cover and store in cool, dry location.

Two Minute Microwave Fudge

Keeps well for a month–cover tightly and
store in cool dry location
POWER LEVER–HIGH
Makes ¾ pound

**1 1 pound box
confectioner's
(powdered) sugar–
3¾ cups
½ cup cocoa
¼ t. salt
¼ cup milk**

**1 T. vanilla extract
1 stick butter or butter
substitute
1 cup chopped pecans or
walnuts**

1. Butter an 8 x 8 square dish–set aside.
2. In a 1½ quart glass casserole, stir together until well
   blended: sugar, cocoa, salt, milk, and vanilla. This will
   become too thick to mix easily with a spoon. Use hands to
   kneed and mix thoroughly. Slice 1 stick of butter in pieces
   and dot all over top.
3. Microwave on High for 2 minutes.
4. Remove from oven. Beat by hand until smooth. Fold in 1
   cup chopped nuts.
5. Pour into a lightly buttered 8 x 8 inch square dish. Cool.
   Cover and cut into squares when ready to serve.

Heavenly Almond Butter Toffee

Keeps well in airtight container for a month–keep in cool dry location or store in refrigerator.
Makes 2 pounds

2 cups butter (4 sticks) or butter substitute
2½ cups sugar
¼ t. cream of tartar
1 cup slivered almonds

1 6 oz. package Mini semi sweet chocolate morsels
1 6 oz. package chopped pecan pieces

1. Grease with margarine 2 regular size cookie sheets or 1 14 x 18 cookie sheet.
2. Melt butter in a 2 quart saucepan.
3. Add sugar. Raise heat, stirring constantly until mixture begins to bubble around the edges of pan. Reduce heat to a slow boil (medium heat).
4. Add cream of tartar and almonds. Stir constantly until mixture turns a caramel color and reaches a hard crack stage–300 to 310 degrees on a candy thermometer. If you do not have a candy thermometer, drop a tiny bit of the syrup into a small amount of ice water. If syrup is ready, you will hear an audible "crack" when syrup hits the ice water– bend down and put your ear over the glass of water.
5. Pour syrup into the cookie sheets, spreading as thin as possible.
6. Immediately pour chocolate chips on top of the toffee. The heat from the toffee will melt the chips. As chocolate melts, spread with a knife.
7. Sprinkle with pecans and press nuts into candy to stick.
8. Refrigerate until candy is cooled and chocolate is hard. Break into pieces and store in airtight container.

New Orleans Christmas Pralines

Makes 3 dozen

1½ cups white sugar
1½ cups firmly packed
  brown sugar
1 cup evaporated milk
¼ cup butter (½ stick) or
  butter substitute

2 cups pecan halves
1 t. vanilla extract
wax paper

1. Lightly grease with margarine enough wax paper to hold 36 4 inch pralines.
2. In a heavy 2 quart sauce pan, combine white and brown sugars and milk. Stir and bring to a boil.
3. Reduce heat to medium and stir until temperature reaches 228 degrees on a candy thermometer. This will be a *very* soft ball.
4. Add butter and pecan halves, continue cooking, stirring constantly until the temperature reaches 235-236 degrees or a soft ball stage*
5. Remove from heat and stir in vanilla.
6. Beat vigorously by hand until mixture begins to thicken and loses its glossy look.
7. Quickly drop by rounded tablespoons onto greased wax paper.
8. Let stand until firm.
9. Store in an air tight container in a cool, dry location.

*See page 192, step # 4, Chocolate Nut Fudge for directions on soft ball stage.

TASTY NIBBLING TREATS

Toasted Pecans

Makes 1 pound

4 cups pecan halves　　**2 t. butter (or more**
¼ t. salt (optional)　　　　**to taste)**

1. Preheat oven to 300 degrees.
2. Pour pecan halves onto a cookie sheet, sprinkle with salt, and dot with butter.
3. Bake 15- 20 minutes, stirring twice during cooking time.
4. Store in airtight container or freeze.

Toasted Pecans Microwave Method

Makes 1 pound
POWER LEVEL-HIGH

4 cups pecan halves　　**1 T. butter**
¼ t. salt

1. Place pecan halves in a 1½ quart casserole.
2. Sprinkle with salt and dot with butter on top.
3. Microwave on high 5 to 6 minutes, stirring every 2 minutes.
4. Store in an airtight container or freeze.

Caramel Crunch

Keeps in airtight container for one month
Makes 7 cups

**½ cup firmly packed
   brown sugar**
½ cup light corn syrup
**4 T. butter (or butter
   substitute)**

½ t. salt
6 cups Chex cereal
**1½ cups unsalted nuts–
   peanuts or pecans**

1. Preheat oven to 250 degrees.
2. In a heavy saucepan, heat sugar, corn syrup, butter, and salt. Cook until sugar and butter are melted, stirring constantly.
3. Add cereal and nuts, stirring until ingredients are well coated.
4. Spread mixture on a lightly greased cookie sheet and bake 30 minutes at 250 degrees. Stir occasionally while baking.
5. Remove from oven, cool, and store in an airtight container.

Caramel Pop Corn

Make Ahead
Keeps in an airtight container for one month
Makes 6 quarts

6 quarts unsalted popcorn (air popped corn is best)
2 sticks butter or margarine
½ cup either dark or light corn syrup

2 cups firmly packed brown sugar
1 t. soda
1 t. salt
1 t. vanilla
1-2 cups pecan halves (optional)

1. Preheat oven to 250 degrees
2. In a heavy saucepan melt butter.
3. Add sugar and syrup. Stir until boiling. Let boil 5 minutes without stirring.
4. Add soda and vanilla and stir until ingredients are well blended.
5. In a large mixing bowl, pour over popped corn and nuts. Stir until corn and nuts are evenly coated.
6. Spread out on a cookie sheet with sides or any pan large enough to hold popcorn. Bake for 45 minutes at 250 degrees. Stir every 15 minutes.
7. Store in an airtight container.

YULETIDE DRINKS AND JAZZED UP SPIRITS!

Aristocrats of Good Cheer Rating Encores and Repours!

YULETIDE DRINKS

Tasty Alcoholic and Non Alcoholic Drinks for Toasting the Spirit of the Holidays

NOTE: SEE PAGE 230 ON HOW TO CONVERT
ALCOHOLIC BEVERAGES INTO NON ALCOHOLIC
DRINKS RETAINING THE FLAVOR

DECORATIVE ICE MOLD

(for cold punches)

SUGGESTIONS FOR DECORATIONS IN ICE MOLD: Slices of limes, lemons, or oranges; red and green cherries; holly or any kind of shiny greenery interspersed in between the fruit.

1. Select the mold to be used. A ring mold, a decorative metal mold, a small mixing bowl, even a saucepan can be used.
2. Measure amount of water mold will hold and pour into another mixing bowl. Let sit 10-15 minutes, stirring two or three times to break up the air bubbles found in tap water. The mold will be cloudy instead of crystal clear if air bubbles are not removed.
3. Pour a small amount of water in bottom of mold—about ½ inch. Place in freezer until it becomes slushy and partially frozen. Arrange fruit and greenery over this layer. Carefully pour cold water over layer of decorations, return to freezer, and let freeze until slushy. Repeat if mold is deep enough for a second layer. If not, fill to top with water and freeze until hard.
4. To unmold: Wrap a hot, wet towel around mold or run bottom side of mold quickly under hot water, and let slip into punch bowl.

Note: Juice or gingerale called for in recipe can also be used for base of ice mold instead of water.

The Wassail Bowl

Centuries ago in olde England, feudal lords and ladies threw a big Christmas Eve party and called it "wassailing". Sitting around huge tables feasting on venison and flaming plum pudding, they dipped into the wassail bowl to toast each other's health and welfare for the coming year. Loosely translated from Anglo Saxon "wes hal" became "Keep in good health" or "Wish you good fortune". Today, the wassail bowl may be the bowl or cup that holds the liquid or it may be the drink itself...most importantly, it is a delightful custom to be shared by good friends during Christmastide. Here are three recipes.

Wassail Bowl (Potent)

Originally the wassail bowl was composed of a spiced ale. This recipe uses beer for a base while the one following is more the American colonial adaptation of the same drink.

Serves 26-28 in four ounce punch cups

3 quarts beer (12 cups)
2 cups sugar
1 t. freshly grated (if possible) nutmeg
1 t. ground ginger

4 lemon slices
2 cups sherry
1 16 oz. jar whole crab apples, drained
Whole cloves for crab apples

1. Drain crab apples and stud all over with whole cloves.
2. In a large pan or soup kettle, put 1 quart (4 cups) of beer, sugar, nutmeg, ginger, and lemon slices.
3. Cook over medium heat, stirring until sugar dissolves.
4. Add remaining beer, sherry, and crab apples. Simmer slowly for 15 minutes but DO NOT BOIL.
5. To serve—pour mixture into warm punch bowl, float studded apples on top, and surround with holly or greenery.

Wassail Bowl (Puritan)

Serves 16 in 4 oz. punch cups

1 cup fresh lemon juice
2 cups fresh orange juice,
or frozen orange juice
properly diluted
2 cups unsweetened
pineapple juice

2 quarts (8 cups) apple
cider
1 t. whole cloves
1 stick cinnamon
¼ cup sugar

1. Tie cloves and cinnamon in a piece of cheese cloth or a clean, thin handkerchief. If not available, put in pot as is and strain when finished cooking.
2. In a large pan, pour lemon juice, orange juice, pineapple juice, and apple cider. Add cloves and cinnamon.
3. Bring to a simmering boil over medium heat. Cover pan, reduce heat, and simmer on low for one hour.
4. Add sugar, stirring until dissolved. Remove from heat.
5. Serve warm in heated bowl surrounded by holly or Christmas greenery.

Wassail Bowl...Harry's Place

Famous for his Christmas hospitality, this is a different and delicious version of wassail

Makes 10-12 four oz. servings

4 cups apple cider
½ cup firmly packed
**   brown sugar**
½ cup dark rum
¼ cup brandy
1 T. Tripple Sec or any
**   orange flavored liqueur**
¼ t. ground cloves
¼ t. ground cinnamon

⅛ t. ground allspice
½ of a lemon thinly sliced
½ of an orange thinly
**   sliced**
salt to taste (optional)
whipped cream,
**   unsweetened**
freshly grated nutmeg

1. In a saucepan, bring 4 cups apple cider to a boil. Reduce heat and add brown sugar, stirring until dissolved.
2. Remove from heat. Add rum, brandy, Tripple Sec, cloves, cinnamon, allspice, lemon, and orange slices. Stir until all ingredients are well blended. Taste and add salt if needed.
3. Heat the mixture over medium heat (DO NOT BOIL) for 2 to 3 minutes.
4. Pour wassail into wine glasses and top with whipped cream and freshly grated nutmeg.

Eggnog

No Southern Christmas celebration could be complete without a bowl of eggnog. It is probably an adaptation of the English milk punch, but it didn't take the Americans long to adapt it. Remember Mark Twain's adage that "too much of anything is bad, but too much whiskey is just enough!"

Eggnog of the Old South

A rich and extravagant version that is
correspondingly good
Make Ahead
(For those wishing to avoid cream, see "Creamless Eggnog"
page 206
Serves 24 in 4 oz. punch cups

6 egg yolks
¾ cup sugar
½ t. vanilla
¼ t. ground nutmeg
1 cup brandy or rum
1⅓ cups bourbon

3 cups whipping cream (or
half and half), chilled
2 cups whole milk
6 egg whites
6 T. sugar

1. Separate eggs. Set whites aside at room temperature.
2. In a mixing bowl, beat egg yolks until light in color.
3. Gradually add ¾ cup of sugar, vanilla, and nutmeg beating constantly.
4. Stir in brandy or rum, bourbon, cream, and milk.
5. Beat egg whites until they form soft peaks.
6. Gradually add sugar, a tablespoon at a time, beating until stiff, but not dry.
7. Fold into eggnog mixture and serve.

Creamless Eggnog

Less powerful and less fluffy, but a boon to those who wish to avoid cream
Makes 28-30 servings in 4 oz. punch cups

6 whole eggs
2 cups powdered sugar
¼ t. salt
1½ T. vanilla
4 cups evaporated milk
1½ cups water

2 cups rum, brandy,
bourbon or a
combination of above
nutmeg (freshly grated if
possible)

1. Beat eggs until light in color.
2. Graduallly beat in powdered sugar, salt, and vanilla.
3. Stir in evaporated milk, water, and rum, brandy, or bourbon.
4. Cover tightly and let ripen in refrigerator for 24 hours.
5. Stir before serving and sprinkle with freshly grated nutmeg.

Rush Hour Eggnog

Serves 40-44 in 4 oz. punch cups

2 quarts (8 cups)
commercial eggnog
2 cups light rum (optional)
2 cups brandy or bourbon
(optional)

6 egg whites at room
temperature
nutmeg for top (freshly
grated if possible)

1. In a large bowl, mix together eggnog, rum, brandy or bourbon.
2. Whip egg whites until stiff, but not dry.
3. Fold into eggnog mixture.
4. Refrigerate until ready to serve.
5. Lightly sprinkle nutmeg on top of each serving.

Quick Eggnog

(Non Alcoholic)
Serves 16 in 4 oz. punch cups

**2 quarts (8 cups)
commercial eggnog
3 T. plus 1 t. rum flavoring
(optional)**

**6 egg whites, room
temperature
nutmeg for top (freshly
grated if possible)**

1. In a large bowl, mix together eggnog and brandy or rum flavoring.
2. Whip egg whites until stiff, but not dry.
3. Fold into eggnog mixture.
4. Refrigerate until ready to serve.
5. Lightly sprinkle nutmeg on top of each serving.

Irish Coffee

Every Irishman will boast that his way of making Irish Coffee is better, but the key ingredients are still good, fresh coffee, and good, fresh cream plus a good brand of Irish whiskey. And for insomniacs there is Irish Sanka.

Individual Servings
Irish coffee glasses, coffee cups, or wine glasses to accommodate number of guests can be lined up on counter.

1. Fill each with 1 jigger of Irish Whiskey
2. Add 1 to 2 tsp. sugar, depending upon taste. Stir to mix well.
3. Add ½ to 1 cup of strong black coffee within 1" of glass or cup rim, and stir well.
4. Top with whipped cream to produce a thick layer on top of the cup, but not enough to be so heavy it sinks into the liquid below. (Non-dairy whipped topping can be substituted, though less flavorful.)

Yuletide Favorite Punches

There is something especially festive about a punch bowl. If you are fortunate enough to own a beautiful old punch bowl, make it the focal point of your party. Surround it with holly and plenty of punch cups and flank it with lit candles. If you don't have a punch bowl, substitute a good-sized soup tureen or even an attractive mixing bowl or a large copper kettle. Attractive mugs can be substituted for punch cups, especially if you are seving a hot punch.

Cold punch should be served icy cold; hot punchs served HOT, not warm. Keep refilling from the potful simmering on the stove.

The following recipes, both alcoholic and non-alcoholic, are tried and tested "party hits" no matter which you may choose.

Champagne Punch

Can be assembled early in day, covered, adding club soda
and champagne at last minute
Serves 35-40 in 4 oz. punch cups

**2 bottles DRY
  champagne, chilled
1 fifth DRY white wine,
  chilled
1 cup Apricot Brandy
1 cup Tripple Sec**

**1-2 quarts club soda
  (amount of soda used
  depends on how much
  you wish to dilute punch)
Block ice or frozen ice mold**

1. In a large punch bowl, combine white wine, apricot brandy, and Tripple Sec. Stir to mix well. Cover and keep chilled until ready to use.

2. At serving time, add champagne and club soda, stir to blend, and place block ice or decorative ice ring in center of bowl.

3. Surround punch bowl with Christmas greenery.

Mock Pink Champagne Punch

(tasty and champagne-like, but non-spirit)
Serves 14-16 in 4 oz. punch cups

1 cup sugar
1 cup water
1 cup canned grapefruit
juice

1 cup orange juice
⅓ cup grenadine syrup*
1 qt. ginger ale, chilled
Block ice or ice mold

1. Boil sugar and water together for 5 minutes.
2. Cool and pour into large pitcher or punch bowl.
3. Add grapefruit and orange juice. Stir well and refrigerate until well chilled.
4. When ready to serve, add grenadine syrup* and chilled gingerale. Stir.
5. Add block ice or decorative ice mold, page 201, to bowl.
6. Decorate with holly and greenery around base of punch bowl.

* Available at liquor store or gourmet shop

Sparkling Cranberry Punch

(Non alcoholic)
Easy—children love it as well as adults—freezes well
Serves 22-24 in 4 oz. punch cups

2 quarts cranberry juice
cocktail
1 6 oz. can frozen
lemonade, thawed

1 quart gingerale, chilled
block ice or ice mold for
punch bowl

1. Mix cranberry juice and lemonade in pitcher or punch bowl.
2. Refrigerate until ready to serve.
3. Pour in gingerale, stir, and add block of ice or decorative ice mold, see page ____.

Holiday Ice Breaker

Makes 12 cups
or serves 24 with 4 oz. punch cups

1 fifth dry white wine, chilled
2 cups orange juice (fresh preferred)
1 cup Cointreau
1 6 oz. can frozen lemonade, thawed and undiluted

1 quart club soda, chilled
orange slices
maraschino cherries (optional)

1. In a large bowl combine chilled white wine, orange juice, Cointreau, and lemonade. Stir to mix well. Cover and refrigerate until ready to serve.
2. Just before serving add club soda. Stir gently.
3. If serving as a punch, add block ice or decorative ice mold, page 201. Garnish with orange slices floating on top.
4. If serving in individual glasses, spear a maraschino cherry and an orange slice on a toothpick and place on rim of glass.

Hot Mulled Cider

Can be made the day before and refrigerated. Heat before
serving time. Caution—do not boil when reheating.
alcoholic or non alcoholic—tasty either way
Makes 20 cups or serves 40 in 4 oz. punch cups

1 gallon apple cider
2 cups sugar
1 cup orange juice
6 T. lemon juice
4 t. whole allspice

½ T. whole cloves
(48-50 cloves)
12 cinnamon sticks
4 cups brandy (optional)

1. Tie allspice, cloves, and cinnamon sticks in a piece
   of cheese cloth or a thin, clean handerchief. If not
   available, put in pot and then strain at end of cooking time.
2. Place cider, sugar, orange juice, lemon juice, and spices in
   a large pot.
3. Bring to a boil. Reduce heat to medium low, stirring
   occasionally and simmer 10 minutes.
4. Add brandy if desired. Stir and remove from heat.
5. Remove spice bag or strain through a finely meshed
   colander.
6. Serve warm in a punch bowl.

READYING THE HOUSE TO SAY "MERRY, MERRY CHRISTMAS!"

The winter sky with it's shining stars at night…a crackling fire…a wreath on the door…a candle glowing from the window…boughs of evergreen and sprigs of holly–a few well placed decorations that say "WELCOME and A VERY MERRY CHRISTMAS!"

READYING THE HOUSE TO SAY "MERRY, MERRY CHRISTMAS!"

Decorating the Easy Way

For the Center of the Table

Candles add an aura of warmth and a magical glow during the Yuletide Season. The burning of a Yule log, is of course, a Christmas tradition, but for modern homes and apartments which do not have fireplaces, a lovely substitute is a fat red or green candle, large enough to burn from the time lighted to the evening's end.

Mirrored Candlelight

Collect all sizes of candles in the same color, ranging from 6 to 14 inches. An odd number of candles is the most effective. Place on a mirror in the center of the table. Add a tiny bit of greenery in between the candles—let the candlelight reflect in the mirror with just enough greenery to enhance.

Candles on a Tray

Place an odd number of candles, varying heights from 6 to 14 inches on a shiny silver or brass tray. Oblong trays fit better in the center of rectangle tables and a round or square tray for a circular table. Add greenery and holly around the base of each candle, letting enough brass or silver show through to add sheen. No candlesticks? Use a liberal amount of florist clay on bottom of each candle and press down firmly. If clay sticks to tray after decorations are removed, remove by rubbing with a soft cloth soaked in lighter fluid.

A Williamsburg Centerpiece

A tall red candle in a hurricane lamp flanked by a ring of fruit, holly berries, and greenery...no hurricane globe? Then:

1. Fill a low container with wet oasis.

2. Place candle in center.

3. Take a branch of greens, cut branches to desired length, stick in oasis.

4. Arrange holly berries on picks and stick in oasis.

5. Add shiny apples on picks (wax apples if not shiny enough).

To make a permanent arrangement, use a block of styrofoam instead of oasis, secure in container with florist clay. Attach stems of greenery and holly to florist picks and stick in styrofoam.

Reserve small sprigs of greenery and wire to small picks. Stick these standing up between fruit to give a live look. With an ice pick make two holes in bottom of artificial apples (or real apples). Insert florist picks in each hole and stick in styrofoam.

Magnolia Leaves and Shiny Christmas Balls

A combination of magnolia leaves, shiny Christmas balls, baby's breath, and white pine cones…

1. Fill a low dish with wet oasis.

2. Arrange small rosettes of magnolia leaves in dish.

3. Place Christmas balls on florist picks (use floral clay to secure top of pick to hole in ball), nestle in between leaves at different angles to bring importance to the design.

4. Spray cones with a clear varnish to give them sheen.

5. Wire pine cones and baby's breath and insert among leaves and balls.

Elegance and Permanence

A centerpiece to enhance any table

Depending upon size and shape of table, cut out a piece of green styrofoam with a knife in a long, thin rectangle. Make 2 inches smaller in width and length than finished measurement.

With greening pines cover top and sides of styrofoam with artificial greenery, making it as flat as possible.

Secure pieces of pine (longest length should be for ends and short pieces for sides and top) to floral short (2 inch) picks. Insert in styrofoam to make a flowing, airy form.

Lastly add decor–holly, twisted velvet ribbon throughout, tiny gold ornaments, small shiny Christmas balls —use anything that compliments your color scheme and your decor. Place candles at either end and in contours of arrangement.

For the Front Door or Over the Fireplace

A beautiful wreath that lasts for years…and years…

New on the market and so simple to use—purchase a Handi-craft Wire Wreath form—12″ up to 20″. Use either artificial, live greenery, or fabric. Simply clip it in and when base is completed, decorate with decor of your choice. Can also be used for centerpieces.

How to Make a Permanent Wreath

Purchase:
Styrofoam form that is reinforced with thin steel wires running throughout (a 10 inch form makes an 18 inch wreath; an 18 inch form makes a 26 inch wreath)
Greening pins
Florist wire

2 and 3 inch floral picks
artificial greenery of good quality
pine cones
ribbon for bow
decorations for wreath: birds, satin balls, Christmas ornaments, dried flowers, holly, dried pods, fruit, etc.

1. Make a hanger with a piece of heavy twine. Leave at least an inch or two at top to fit over nail. Secure with greening pins.
2. Pin greenery to cover wreath form, making as flat as possible.

Greening pin

3. Wire pine cones with florist wire and then with picks–insert around outside of wreath form.

4. Wire boughs of greenery with floral picks. Cut lengths an inch longer than length of pine cones. Insert between cones, covering well space in between. Use 3″ picks for outside cones.

5. Cut shorter pieces of greenery, wire to 2 inch picks and insert on top of wreath form, covering all holes.

6. Wire decorations of your choice and insert pick into wreath form at desired angles.

Continued on next page

7. Make bow, page 224, and secure with pick. Insert at desired position.

8. Fill in any holes and hang.

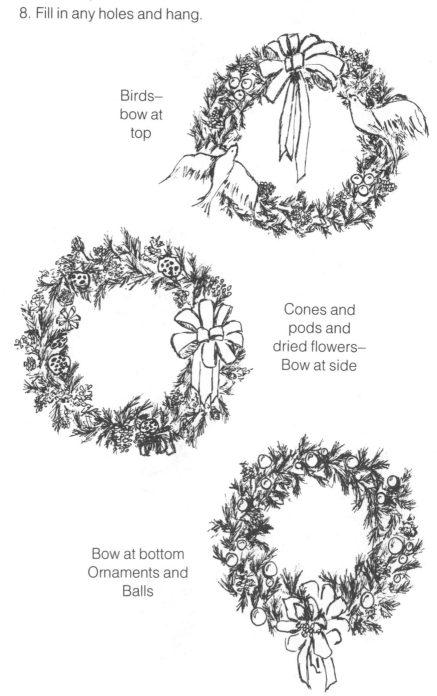

Birds—
bow at
top

Cones and
pods and
dried flowers—
Bow at side

Bow at bottom
Ornaments and
Balls

Grape Vine Wreath

grapevines
pine cones
**dried flowers or Christmas
   figures**

baby's breath
ribbon bow
florist wire

1. Soak vines until pliable.
2. Shape into circle desired diameter. Use florist wire to secure vines.
3. Wire pine cones, dried flowers, baby's breath and insert them among openings in grapevines–run wire through wreath and secure by twisting in back.
4. Make large bow page 224, place at top, bottom, or angle at side and secure with wire inserted through wreath and tied in back.

Decorative Bows

A large, elegant bow at the end of the staircase (lush velvet or country plaid depending on decor of the home), a tiny satin bow on a small candlestick; a perkey bow on an accessory that is used all year can turn that piece into a very special Christmas decoration. Bows are versatile! The following directions are for a large bow–decrease yardage and width of ribbon for smaller bows, following same directions.

Buy 3 yards ribbon, 2 to 3 inches wide.

1. Measure 18 inches from end of ribbon. Hold the end of the ribbon wilth your right hand, and hold at the 18 inch mark with your left hand. Release ribbon from right hand. Place right hand above left hand on ribbon and twist. After twisting, ribbon hanging down will be right side up, while ribbon above twist will have wrong side out.

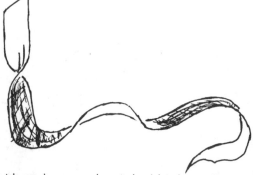

2. Place right hand approximately 4 inches above the twist and loop it towards you. With your left hand, hold the loop. With your right hand, twist the ribbon below your left thumb. This will make your first loop in the middle and become your center bow loop.

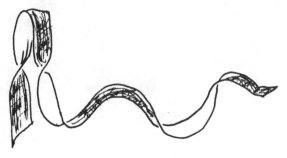

3. Work loops up and down from center loop, twisting each time. Make each loop slightly larger than the last loop.

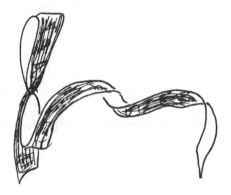

4. Make about 5 loops up and 5 loops down for finished bow. Secure with a florist wire. If a longer, additional center tail is desired, cut a piece of ribbon 1 inch longer than tails, twist at top and wrap with wire. Attach in back at center of bow.

Baskets

Baskets are an atttractive Christmas decoration—on a fireplace hearth, in the kitchen, a centerpiece on a table—anywhere a touch of greenery is needed to say Merry Christmas!

1. Use fresh or artificial greenery. If using fresh, place a low container with wet oasis in bottom of basket. Cut greenery to a sharp point on ends and stick in oasis.
   If artificial—cut a block of green styrofoam to fit in bottom of basket. Secure with floral clay. Wire greenery to picks and insert in styrofoam.

2. Spray pine cones with a clear varnish and wire with florist picks. Stick in basket at different angles for interesting design.

3. Add final touches—holly, baby's breath, artificial cranberries tied with a bow, shiny red apples selected for color and long stems. Tie apple stems with ribbon ½ inch wide and 8 inches long—cut ends with a W shape. Place a few bundles of cinnamon sticks tied together with a ribbon in between the apples. (See page 217 on inserting floral picks into apples)

Quick Decorating Idea

Buy a roll of ribbon in Christmas colors. Make bows with a sprig of artificial holly or line in the center. Tie around the neck of your children's special stuffed animals and place under the tree, on a few steps of the stairs—or any other niche that needs a special touch of Christmas!

Setting the Scene

The Basics

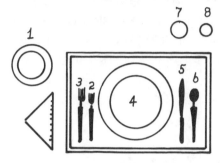

(1) Salad Plate (2) Salad Fork (3) Dinner Fork
(4) Dinner Plate (5) Dinner Knife (6) Teaspoon*
(7) Water Glass (8) Wine Glass*

* May be omitted

Basics Elaborated

(1) Salad Fork (2) Dinner Fork
(3) Dinner Plate (4) Dinner Knife
(5) Teaspoon (6) Soup Spoon*
(7) Wine Glass (8) Water Glass (9) Bread and Butter plate
(10) Bread and Butter knife (11) Salad Plate

* If serving soup as first course

Important Rules

FOR CONGEALING SALADS

1. Use 1 T. or 1 envelope plain gelatin to 2 cups liquid.
2. Soak 1 T. gelatin in ¼ cup cold water for about 2-3 minutes to soften or until gelatin has absorbed all the liquid.
3. Add gelatin to 1¾ cups boiling water or juice and stir until dissolved.

TO DOUBLE GELATIN RECIPES

1. Instead of using 4 cups of liquid, reduce to 3¾ cups total liquid if single recipe calls for 2 cups.

MOLDING AND UNMOLDING CONGEALED SALADS

1. Spray molds with a "no stick" cooking spray or lightly oil mold before adding salad.
2. To unmold: moisten outside of mold with warm water until salad is loose from sides and bottom. Hold plate beneath mold and invert onto plate.
3. NO SALAD MOLDS? Use paper cups or short fat juice glasses for individual molds. Use mixing bowls or a cooking pan for larger molds.

HOW TO HARD-COOK AN EGG

1. Place eggs in sauce pan.
2. Cover with cold water.
3. Place pan on medium high heat and cover.
4. Bring water to a boil.
5. Reduce heat and let water simmer for 17-18 minutes.
6. Immediately run cold water over cooked eggs to stop cooking process.

Conversion Chart for Using Imitation Rum, Brandy, or Sherry Instead of Alcohol

FOR BRANDY:
1 part imitation Brandy extract equals 5 parts good quality Brandy

FOR RUM:
2 T. imitation Rum extract equals 1 T. dark Rum
1 T. imitation Rum extract equals 5 T. light Rum

FOR SHERRY:
Use equal amounts of imitation Sherry for real Sherry

Measurements, Weights, Equivalents

MEASUREMENTS THAT HELP

3 teaspoons	=	1 tablespoon
2 tablespoons	=	1 ounce
4 tablespoons	=	¼ cup
8 tablespoons	=	½ cup
4 ounces	=	½ cup
16 tablespoons	=	1 cup
8 ounces	=	1 cup
1 cup	=	½ pint
2 cups	=	1 pint
16 ounces	=	1 pound
2 pints	=	1 quart
4 cups	=	1 quart
4 quarts	=	1 gallon

METRIC CONVERSION TABLE
WEIGHT

To Change	To	Multiply by
Ounces	Grams	30.0
Pounds	Kilograms	.48

VOLUME

To Change	To	Multiply by
Teaspoons	Milliliters	5.0
Tablespoons	Milliliters	15.0
Cups	Milliliters	250.0
Cups	Liters	.25
Pints	Liters	.5
Quarts	Liters	1.0
Gallons	Liters	4.0

LENGTH

To Change	To	Multiply by
Inches	Millimeters	25.0
Inches	Centimeters	2.5
Feet	Centimeters	30.0
Yards	Meters	0.9

LIQUID MEASUREMENTS*
(nearest convenient equivalents)

1T	=	15 ml.
¼ cup	=	62.5 ml.
⅓ cup	=	83.3 ml.
½ cup	=	125 ml.
1 cup	=	250 ml. (¼ liter)
2 cups	=	500 ml. (½ liter)
1 quart	=	1,000 ml. (1 liter)
1 gallon	=	4,000 ml. (4 liters)

WEIGHTS

(nearest convenient equivalents)

½ ounce	=	15 grams
1 ounce	=	30 grams
4 ounces (¼ lb.)	=	114 grams
8 ounces (½ lb.)	=	227 grams
16 ounces (1 lb.)	=	464 grams

Note to remember:

100 grams is slightly less than ¼ lb.
250 grams is slightly more than ½ lb.
500 grams is slightly more than 1 lb.
1,000 grams is slightly more than 2 lbs. or 1 kilogram

* Taken from "Units of Weights and Measures", U.S.
  Government Printing Office, Washington, D.C.

AVERAGE CAN SIZES

Can Size	Weight	Cupfuls
8 oz.	8 oz.	1
No. 1	11 oz.	1⅓
No. 1½	16 oz.	2
No. 2	20 oz.	2½
No. 2½	28 oz.	3½
No. 3	33 oz.	4
No. 10	106 oz.	13

HELPFUL EQUIVALENTS

1 stick butter	½ cup
2 cups butter	1 pound
1 square chocolate	1 ounce
1 lemon	2-3 T. juice
2 cups diced meat	1 pound meat
½ cup rice	2 cups cooked rice
9 saltines crushed	1 cup crumbs
3 medium apples	1 pound or 2⅓ cups
1 cup grated cheese	¼ pound or 4 ounces

INDEX

It's Christmas!   **Rush Hour Superchef**   **Rush Hour Times Two!**

Mail to: DEANNE II, INC.
          #3 Quail Run, Rt. 4
          Carthage, MO 64836

Please send ____ copies of IT'S CHRISTMAS!   @ 12.95 each _____
Please send ____ copies of RUSH HOUR
    SUPERCHEF   @ 12.95 each _____
MO residents please add sales tax   @   .77 each _____
Postage and handling   @ 2.50 each _____
                                            @ 3.50 for 2 books _____

Please send ____ copies of RUSH HOUR
    TIMES TWO!   @ 7.95 each _____
MO residents please add sales tax   @   .47 each _____
Postage and handling   @ 1.75 each _____
                                            @ 2.50 for 2 books _____

Autograph to read: _____
_____   TOTAL _____

☐ Check ☐ Money Order ☐ Visa or Mastercard (see over)
Make Check or money order payable to DEANNE II, INC.
Name_____
Address _____
City _____ State _____ Zip _____
Telephone: 417-358-7814   **Fax 417-358-4817**

It's Christmas!   **Rush Hour Superchef**   **Rush Hour Times Two!**

Mail to: DEANNE II, INC.
          #3 Quail Run, Rt. 4
          Carthage, MO 64836

Please send ____ copies of IT'S CHRISTMAS!   @ 12.95 each _____
Please send ____ copies of RUSH HOUR
    SUPERCHEF   @ 12.95 each _____
MO residents please add sales tax   @   .77 each _____
Postage and handling   @ 2.50 each _____
                                            @ 3.50 for 2 books _____

Please send ____ copies of RUSH HOUR
    TIMES TWO!   @ 7.95 each _____
MO residents please add sales tax   @   .47 each _____
Postage and handling   @ 1.75 each _____
                                            @ 2.50 for 2 books _____

Autograph to read: _____
_____   TOTAL _____

☐ Check ☐ Money Order ☐ Visa or Mastercard (see over)
Make Check or money order payable to DEANNE II, INC.
Name_____
Address _____
City _____ State _____ Zip _____
Telephone: 417-358-7814   **Fax 417-358-4817**

It's Christmas! **Rush Hour Superchef** **Rush Hour Times Two!**

If using Visa or MasterCard, please fill in the following:

Name_____

Address_____ Phone (_____)_____

City_____ State_____ Zip_____

Charge to my: ☐ **VISA** Visa ☐ MasterCard MasterCard

Account Number: ┌─┬─┬─┬─┬─┬─┬─┬─┬─┬─┬─┬─┬─┬─┬─┬─┬─┬─┬─┐

Expiration Date:_____
(Month)   (Year)

Customer's Signature_____

It's Christmas! **Rush Hour Superchef** **Rush Hour Times Two!**

If using Visa or MasterCard, please fill in the following:

Name_____

Address_____ Phone (_____)_____

City_____ State_____ Zip_____

Charge to my: ☐ **VISA** Visa ☐ MasterCard MasterCard

Account Number: ┌─┬─┬─┬─┬─┬─┬─┬─┬─┬─┬─┬─┬─┬─┬─┬─┬─┬─┬─┐

Expiration Date:_____
(Month)   (Year)

Customer's Signature_____

DEANNE II, INC.

#3 Quail Run, Rt. 4   •   Carthage, Missouri 64836

It's Christmas!   **Rush Hour Superchef**   **Rush Hour Times Two!**

Mail to: DEANNE II, INC.
        #3 Quail Run, Rt. 4
        Carthage, MO 64836

Please send ____ copies of IT'S CHRISTMAS!   @ 12.95 each _____
Please send ____ copies of RUSH HOUR
   SUPERCHEF   @ 12.95 each _____
MO residents please add sales tax   @ .77 each _____
Postage and handling   @ 2.50 each _____
                                        @ 3.50 for 2 books _____

Please send ____ copies of RUSH HOUR
   TIMES TWO!   @ 7.95 each _____
MO residents please add sales tax   @ .47 each _____
Postage and handling   @ 1.75 each _____
                                        @ 2.50 for 2 books _____

Autograph to read: _____

_____ TOTAL _____

☐ Check   ☐ Money Order   ☐ Visa or Mastercard (see over)

Make Check or money order payable to DEANNE II, INC.

Name_____

Address _____

City _____ State _____ Zip _____

Telephone: 417-358-7814   **Fax 417-358-4817**

It's Christmas!   **Rush Hour Superchef**   **Rush Hour Times Two!**

Mail to: DEANNE II, INC.
        #3 Quail Run, Rt. 4
        Carthage, MO 64836

Please send ____ copies of IT'S CHRISTMAS!   @ 12.95 each _____
Please send ____ copies of RUSH HOUR
   SUPERCHEF   @ 12.95 each _____
MO residents please add sales tax   @ .77 each _____
Postage and handling   @ 2.50 each _____
                                        @ 3.50 for 2 books _____

Please send ____ copies of RUSH HOUR
   TIMES TWO!   @ 7.95 each _____
MO residents please add sales tax   @ .47 each _____
Postage and handling   @ 1.75 each _____
                                        @ 2.50 for 2 books _____

Autograph to read: _____

_____ TOTAL _____

☐ Check   ☐ Money Order   ☐ Visa or Mastercard (see over)

Make Check or money order payable to DEANNE II, INC.

Name_____

Address _____

City _____ State _____ Zip _____

Telephone: 417-358-7814   **Fax 417-358-4817**

It's Christmas!   **Rush Hour Superchef**   **Rush Hour Times Two!**

If using Visa or MasterCard, please fill in the following:

Name_____

Address_____ Phone_(_____)_____

City_____ State_____ Zip_____

Charge to my: ☐ [VISA] Visa   ☐ [MasterCard] MasterCard

Account Number: [ ][ ][ ][ ][ ][ ][ ][ ][ ][ ][ ][ ][ ][ ][ ][ ][ ]

Expiration Date:_____
                (Month)   (Year)

Customer's Signature_____

It's Christmas!   **Rush Hour Superchef**   **Rush Hour Times Two!**

If using Visa or MasterCard, please fill in the following:

Name_____

Address_____ Phone_(_____)_____

City_____ State_____ Zip_____

Charge to my: ☐ [VISA] Visa   ☐ [MasterCard] MasterCard

Account Number: [ ][ ][ ][ ][ ][ ][ ][ ][ ][ ][ ][ ][ ][ ][ ][ ][ ]

Expiration Date:_____
                (Month)   (Year)

Customer's Signature_____

DEANNE II, INC.

#3 Quail Run, Rt. 4   •   Carthage, Missouri 64836